Underdog

Underdog

TRAINING THE MUTT, MONGREL AND MIXED BREED AT HOME

Mordecai Siegal *and* Matthew Margolis

 STEIN AND DAY/*Publishers*/New York

First published in 1974
Copyright © 1974 by Mordecai Siegal and Matthew Margolis
Library of Congress Catalog No. 73–82568
All rights reserved
Designed by David Miller
Printed in the United State of America
Stein and Day/*Publishers*/Scarborough House, Briarcliff Manor, N.Y. 10510
ISBN 0–8128–1615–3

SECOND PRINTING, 1974

*This book is dedicated to
the men and women of the Humane Society
of the United States and all
those who champion the underdog!*

CONTENTS

ACKNOWLEDGMENTS

About the training pictures—Many thanks to Linda Steigner, professional trainer for the National Institute of Dog Training, Inc. A tip of the collapsible top hat to Bruce Renick, director of training for that organization.

To photographer Mark Handler who once again has proved his artistic wit and skill this second time around. All photographs depicting obedience training are the result of his fine work.

To Mr. and Mrs. Otto Preminger, their son Marc, and their daughter Victoria for permitting us to photograph *Spaghetti*. To Harold Sclar and *Herschel*. To Bonnie Shalin and *Butch*. To Bruce Lowitt and *Connie*. To Sandy Capelli and *Sir Gregory*.

About the pictures for "Mutts of Distinction"—Our sincere gratitude to Barbara Austin, Leonard Brook, and Bunny Brook of the Dawn Animal Agency of New York City.

With appreciation to Anita Schneiderman for her very special assistance.

Thank you to Wally Exman for many reasons.

The authors wish to acknowledge admiration for and appreciation of the many dedicated staff members of the Humane Society of the United States and the valuable service they perform. In particular a special thank you to Guy R. Hodge, director of investigations; to Patrice Jones of the information and legislation department;

and to Phyllis Wright, executive director of The National Humane Education Center. Through their effort and cooperation we have been able to present the Directory of Animal Adoption Agencies.

Appreciation to Bob Greenfield of A-1 House of Trophies.

And a special, warm thanks to Vicki Siegal for the many arduous hours spent on this project.

PREFACE

In war, politics, and sports an underdog is a team, a candidate, or a side whose inferior position appeals to our sense of fair play and justice. Considering that the underdog helps us to choose sides, what is more natural than wanting the disadvantaged to come out on top? It is no play on words to refer to mutts, mongrels, and mixed breeds as underdogs when one considers that there are virtually millions upon millions of them sitting in animal shelters everywhere waiting for adoption. It is the fervent purpose of this book to encourage the many potential dog owners to take a mutt home and save his life.

Throughout the training chapters of this book you will find many photographs illustrating the various techniques of dog training. You may also notice that the trainers are dressed in white tie, tails, and, where appropriate, gowns. If members of the Dog Fancy can attire themselves in formal wear during the finals of Westminster, Chicago International, or England's Crufts, then certainly the least we can do for the ordinary mutt is to give him this one display of sartorial splendor and a tip of the collapsible top hat.

To further demonstrate our celebration of the ordinary dog we have included a chapter entitled "Mutts of Distinction," which is a photo gallery of mongrel dogs that have earned a place in the sun through their own unique abilities or those of their special owners. Mutts can be glamorous, too.

But this is essentially a dog training book. A "how to . . ." Dog training is usually thought of in a frivolous light and not without some justification. It is one of the lesser arts. It is an inescapable fact, however, that a trained dog usually lives with kind, intelligent, and lively human beings. To train a dog is really to develop a full relationship with him. To enjoy such a relationship is to feel less alone in the world and more a part of it in the largest sense imaginable. To rescue a mongrel and then train it may or may not be a noble gesture. Such things are determined elsewhere. Within this context, however, dog training, in its small way, makes a contribution to the enrichment of our lives. To live with a dog is certainly to be on the side of life and all that is real.

Underdog

1

I'M A MUTT—YOU'RE A MUTT

No dogs allowed without proper papers,
No cure for the common cur.
"No mutts, if you please," said the let-'em-eat-cakers,
"Can't stand that mixed colored fur."

But Darwin still haunts us with graven glee,
He smirks in the ghostly fog.
"Bananas and trees are man's pedigree,
He's just one more underdog!"

—M. S.

IN A DOG'S WORLD real-estate values would never go down simply because a Rottweiler moved into the neighborhood. If dogs held dominion, country clubs would be open to Puli, Cocker, Basenji, and Mongrel alike. No living species is more democratic in spirit and tolerant in nature than the domestic dog. When a common cur and a West Highland White Terrier encounter each other the same thing happens as if they were born in the same litter. They look, they sniff, they tussle, and walk away pleased with themselves, cherishing the memories of ancient rituals performed and tastes and smells experienced. No one would ask to see their papers and establish proof of physical purity. All things being equal, the ordinary mutt would have his day.

America is a nation of mutts; which is to say, a nation that placed a want ad in the hellholes of the world and invited the wretched of every conceivable culture to leap into the star-spangled blender and purée into *sauce américaine.* What came out was a mixture of people who created a society quite distinct from its dozens of *purebred* forebears. This ethnic and cultural mix finds its parallel in the world of the dog. There are more than 34 million dogs in the United States living with families. One and a half million of them are registered with the American Kennel Club as purebred. However, over 30 million are mongrels or mixed breeds. That's a lot of mutts. Obviously, it takes one to love one.

Training a mutt is just as important as training the most exotic of the purebreds. After all, DeClive-Lowe's Beau Geste of Studly Man-or Estates is just as likely to take a squirt on the living-room carpet as Spot Siegal. Good old Beau Geste and his lower-in-status pal Spot both need housebreaking and the lifesaving benefits of obedience training.

This is a book that is primarily concerned with training. However, as the title indicates, training can be somewhat different when applied to dogs of indeterminate breed origins. Every pure breed has predictable temperament characteristics that let you know what you're up against in the training process. With a mutt it's anyone's guess—unless you know how to evaluate the dog's temperament. That is precisely what you will learn in the coming chapters. Imagine your Harvey, half St. Bernard, half Greyhound, being trained to "Come When Called" off-leash, outdoors. Will he want to chase the first thing that resembles a mechanical rabbit or simply lumber up to you and offer a shot of brandy? Is he nervous, shy, lethargic, even-tempered, or completely unpredictable? These are important things when applying the techniques of obedience training.

The desire to train a dog implies that a relationship either exists or is desired on the part of the owner. The pleasures of dog ownership depend very much on the relationship between the dog and his "family." Therefore, it is extremely useful to understand what exists between the average dog owner and the ordinary dog. Why do you own a mutt? The answer to that question may affect your attitude toward the dog and may even improve your relationship with him. This can only enhance the training program you are about to begin.

Many mutt-owning clients of the National Institute of Dog

Training, Inc., were sent questionnaires. They were asked if they deliberately chose a mongrel in preference to a purebred dog, and if so, why. Here are some of those answers:

▶   I am very much opposed to deliberately breeding more dogs into the world while thousands of good mutts are left homeless, unloved, and unwanted.

▶   The initial cost is cheaper. They are supposedly less temperamental. Also, I get tired of people trotting out the pedigree of their dog. A dog is a dog, and is no less loving or devoted because it does or doesn't have "papers." What matters is the dog itself and its basic qualities.

▶   We found him!

▶   Mongrels are healthier and smarter. They require no care.

▶   Because we have always known mongrels and considered them more psychologically balanced than purebreds. Champ was only a twenty-dollar investment and has never been ill, is affectionate, wildly enthusiastic and has paid us back our investment three million times over.

▶   We found our dog in the park, thought it cruel to leave any dog. He is a very adorable mongrel as they all are.

▶   I wanted a dog we could love and not have to worry about his frailness or idiosyncrasies.

▶   My boys wanted a dog desperately—a Beagle like Snoopy, to be exact. I did make some vague inquiries about purebreds but felt the anxiety I would feel about taking care of a dog that had cost me that much money wasn't worth it, so I went to the ASPCA and took the dog that looked most like a Beagle.

▶   I acquired my first mixed breed from Bide-a-Wee when my children were small and I was broke. I wanted a Beagle and got a Beagle-type. She was *so* magnificent—intelligent, sensitive, loving, funny—that we wanted to perpetuate the characteristics. So we mated her (like we had a choice!) with her German Shepherd lover. We now have our third generation (the second born at home). The German Shepherd–Beagle mated with a Doberman-Beagle. The third generation is better than the first. The father and son we now have are great watchdogs, loyal, gentle with children, intelligent to an almost eerie extent, and certainly as handsome as any purebred I've seen.

Of the many, many responses to the questionnaire none was more articulate or informative than that from Mrs. D. Anderson of Floral Park, New York. She wrote:

> All I wanted was a dog—someone who barks at one end and wags at the other—uncropped, undocked, no papers—just a dog. I have nothing against purebred dogs—they're beautiful. It's people's attitudes that bother me. "I have a purebred! " "Oh, it's a mutt . . ." So what? It's still a dog. It will still jump on people, bark at the mailman, and be good company on a walk no matter who its parents are. The only papers a *dog* needs are under him. Mutts are all too often looked down on as unworthy.
> We found Sheba at the West Hampton Bide-a-Wee last April. She's a Collie-Afghan and her mother taught her well. She sat with her back against the gate, looking over her shoulder. One look at those brown doleful eyes (I didn't see the mischief behind them) and I was hooked. She's a healthy, responsive dog with a sweetheart temperament, everything I wanted in a dog. She will fill my desire, and all for only eight dollars! At the moment she's asleep with her nose in my lap. I know she doesn't belong on the couch but I love it!
> Sincerely, Nikki Anderson.

There are several basic reasons that turn certain people in the direction of mutt ownership and these reasons are quite available in the answers to our questionnaire. Probably the greatest reason for the interest in mutts is economics. Because of the three largest dog shows in the world (Crufts, London; Westminster, New York; and International, Chicago), the purebred dog business has expanded beyond the old limits of well-to-do fanciers. The 1.5 million purebreds that the American Kennel Club registers each year represent many million of dollars in over-the-counter sales of specialized puppies. The purchase price of a purebred puppy ranges anywhere between $100 and $1,000, a rather expensive luxury for the average family. This figure, of course, does not include medical expenses, food bills, equipment, professional training, books, vitamins, and many other items. All this makes the pet industry one of the largest contributors to the gross national product in the past ten years. The cost of the purebred puppy represents the largest expenditure the pet owner makes. Because of these economic facts of life many who desire a dog are discovering what others have known all along—the lovable mutt is every bit as affectionate and useful, satisfies every desire, and costs less than $25. (Often the puppy is free.)

Many people find it very difficult to identify with a purebred animal. The acquisition of a dog is very much like the acquisition of a painting. There are large personal implications attached to what kind of painting (or dog) one takes into one's home. By exercising their taste in public many people have revealed a little bit of their private selves. The person who refers to his "mutt" may very likely see himself as one who has come from a humble background or one with humble tastes. In that instance the dog becomes an extension of the owner. A purebred dog would interfere with that self-concept and make the owner uncomfortable. It would be like employing a live-in butler for a six-room house in the suburbs. The relationship is forced and then deteriorates in a short period of time. The terms "mongrel" and "mixed breed" might even have racial overtones with both positive and negative feelings attached to them.

What better demonstration against the notion of snobbery than to trot out an ordinary dog, no papers, no pedigree, no distinctive breed features beyond a white tail and a black spot over one eye. Because so many breeds are owned for reasons of ostentation or status the mutt can very easily help his owner make a statement of democratic principles.

Acquiring a mutt can also make the owner feel that he has done something useful, something humane, something elevating and good for the soul. There are few who can walk through the kennel area of an animal shelter and not be moved at the sight of one or two hundred dogs, confined in small cages, waiting for adoption or execution. There are those who believe that Man and all other living things are bound together in an interdependent community and to allow the suffering or death of a living creature is destructive and alienating for all concerned. That type of mutt owner feels that he is acting on his good impulses and enjoys the feeling. Like an ex-con helping a friend get out of jail, this owner is rescuing a life and feels most strongly that it matters.

Of course, every town and city has its fair share of animal collectors who somehow manage to acquire more animals than people. It is not hard to pick out the house that is accommodating eighteen cats and eleven dogs. All that canned tuna and cracked barley. Still, that person, drunk on the milk of human kindness, is preferable to the sunshine patriarch who loves 'em in July and abandons 'em in September.

There are many reasons to own a mutt but the best one is simply that you want a dog. It would be a gross injustice to say that there was no purpose to the purebred animal. The pursuit of genetic predictability and a striving for physical perfection, beauty, temperament, and utility are worthwhile goals. But for those who want to enjoy the pleasures of a cheerful companion and a loving being, a playmate, a pal, a teacher of the life process, a source of heartbreak and joy, then the common dog, like the common man, will do just fine. If this makes sense to you, then you have just joined the Cult of the Underdog.

2

A DOG FOR ALL SEASONS
An Introduction to Training

IF YOU HAVE OWNED your dog more than four weeks it is quite possible that you are not on speaking terms with him. By this time he has probably chewed up your favorite slipper, knocked over countless bags of trash, stained the carpet, nipped your finger, kept you awake with his howling, and in general made himself a nuisance. On the other hand the dog has probably recoiled in fear at your hollering, runs the minute you reach for your newspaper, ducks under the bed at the sight of the leash and collar, and tries to hide his snout from you after messing on the living-room floor. You see, he's as weary of you as you are of him. If we were talking about newlyweds it would be time for one of you to go home to mother (or the divorce court). Many marriage counselors would suggest that the failure to communicate is the cause for most conjugal strife. The same applies to dogs and their owners. In the case of pet ownership, obedience training is the most workable solution to that problem. It is not recommended for married couples.

Training a dog is the only civilized answer to living with one. All the hollering you are capable of, and all the smacking and swatting you can deliver, will never get an animal to behave like an adult human being (a questionable goal). The best one can hope for is an animal who has been taught when he may and may not respond to his impulses. That's it. But that is quite a lot to get from a dog. He may be taught where and when he may urinate, when he may bark, what he may eat, where he may sit or lie down, where and how to walk, etc. And all this is available if the calm, loving, generous, intelligent owner knows how to communicate his wishes to the dog. What the authors of this book hope to accomplish is to teach the average pet owner how to communicate with his dog. This ideal state will not come about without effort, patience, and the desire to do the work. However, the rewards are priceless. You may experience ten to fifteen years of pleasure that a loving, joyful relationship can bring. A dog is fun. A dog is love. All the rest is commerce.

A PHILOSOPHY OF TRAINING

There are two basic elements that distinguish this obedience course from most others, especially those from the dark and vague past. The first is an attempt to determine the temperament of your nonspecified breed of dog so that the training may be suited to his temperament limitations. This is exactly what a professional dog trainer does when he first meets your animal. Armed with this information he can best determine how to handle the animal.

The second element is the removal of the word *punishment* from your training lexicon. This is no small matter. We do not believe that a dog should live out his days as if he were in penal servitude on Devil's Island. Not even Count Dracula rubbed the dog's nose in his own urine or excretion nor did the Frankenstein monster point an accusing finger and say, "Shame, shame." Hitting, hollering, or accusing fingers accomplish nothing in dog training. It only helps create a neurotic dog whose behavior may force you to get rid of him. And let us put away, once and for all, the *school-of-journalism* technique that demands a slap from a rolled-up newspaper. It wins no Pulitzer Prize here—not even if you merely strike it against your own hand. The use of a newspaper will only cause a deep-embedded fear of long, cylindrical objects in the mind of your dog. Punishing a dog makes him live in a state of fear, terror, and uncertainty. Because punishing is not teaching, the animal never learns what it is that you want. The end result is that you never get what you want.

Be kind, be affectionate, be firm. These are the kingpins that hold up the entire structure of this training course. When a dog does not behave properly or refuses to obey a command he has been taught, he is "corrected"—not "punished." Each and every time the dog does respond properly he is rewarded—with praise—nothing else. Because most dogs desire to be accepted and loved they will always work for your praise. It is the giving and withholding of this praise that is the most valuable teaching tool in obedience training.

Living with a dog should be like living in one of those European duchies where the owner is the Monarch and the dog is the loyal subject. You, the Grand Duke, are benevolent, generous, but firm in making things run smoothly. Your loyal subject, Ralph, obeys your clear, concise orders without question and is generously rewarded for doing so. Although dog ownership shouldn't be totalitarian in nature, it isn't exactly ideal as a constitutional democracy, either. A dog is a simple creature who wants to be shown what to do because there are many things he cannot do for himself.

WHEN TO START THE TRAINING

Among the many misconceptions that exist in dog training and ownership is the one about the age requirement for training. There are still many people who hold the notion that a dog must not be trained until he is at least six months old. Many fix the time at one year old. The principal reason for this misconception has to do with the kind of training that once was available. Up until a few years ago the only way a dog could be trained professionally was to send him to a kennel type of school where the dog is mixed in with many others. Because the dog cannot be immunized for rabies until he is six months old he could not be "sent away" for training. Somehow the idea of waiting six months before training got away from the vaccination part of the story and became a fixed rule. Nowadays many professional trainers come to the home and work with the dog in his own environment, thus obviating the need to wait. It is unnecessary for owners of large dogs to live with an animal who defecates on the floor and chews the furniture the minute he is left alone, simply because he is not yet six months old.

You may train any puppy once he has reached eight weeks. If you start at that age the dog will be completely housebroken and obedient by the time he is four or five months old. We consider this the ideal situation. Among the many obvious advantages the most important one has to do with the owner's not giving up the dog out of frustration and thus dooming the animal to an uncertain future. One need only walk through an animal shelter to see a representation of the living statistics. When dogs are given up or abandoned, most of them will either starve to death, die in traffic, or be executed by some government institution. Comparatively, very few find their way back to a decent home. Training at eight weeks is the best time. According to recent scientific studies in dog behavior, eight weeks is not only possible but it is desirable.

In his book, *The New Knowledge of Dog Behavior,* Clarence J. Pfaffenberger, of Guide Dogs for the Blind, of San Rafael, California, writes of his research with Dr. J. P. Scott of the Roscoe B. Jackson Memorial Laboratory in Bar Harbor, Maine. According to Dr. Scott a puppy has no capacity for learning until his twenty-first day of life. At that point his mental and nervous capacities develop at a very rapid rate and influence his abilities to relate with man and animal indelibly for life. (It is at this age that a puppy begins to eliminate without the aid of the mother.) He further states that at seven weeks of age a puppy's brain waves indicate they are those of a fully mature dog. By the eighth week the dog is capable simultaneously of being weaned and transferred to a new owner. The new owner may then enforce an easy style of discipline through obedience training and housebreaking. If the new owner expresses a great deal of attention and affection the puppy will adjust with great ease. By the time the dog is sixteen weeks old it has already begun the behavior that will continue throughout its life.

Pfaffenberger states:

> In the time, at three weeks of age, when the learning stage began, to sixteen weeks of age, the character of a dog is formed. No

matter how good his inherited character traits, if they are not given a chance of expression during this period he will never be as good a dog as he could have been

... from forty-nine to eighty-four days of age (i.e. seven to twelve weeks), he [Dr. Scott] found to be the best time to form the man-dog relationships, and an attachment by the puppy which will permanently affect the attitude of the dog to human beings and his acceptance of direction and education. Considerable teaching can be done at this time, much as a child in the beginning grades learns things which are to become the foundation of his education.

TRAINING SCHEDULES

An eight-to-twelve-week-old puppy. The training program will last for approximately twelve weeks, depending on the animal's ability to learn, willingness to learn, and temperament. The length of each training session depends on whether the dog is eight, ten, or twelve weeks old. The eight-week-old puppy should be trained once a day, seven days a week, with sessions not more than three to five minutes long. This should be varied depending on the dog's temperament. If he is a very active puppy he can be trained a full five minutes. If he is a passive dog train him no longer than three minutes a session. Give him one session a day, seven sessions a week. By the time he is ten weeks old, if the dog is responding well, give him two sessions a day. This totals fourteen sessions a week. When the puppy is twelve weeks of age continue the sessions at two per day but increase the time length to five minutes a session. The older a puppy gets the more training he can take and the greater are his learning powers.

A three-to-five-month-old puppy. A puppy in this age bracket will take approximately ten weeks to train. Beginning with a three-month-old puppy, start with one session a day, seven days a week, with each session lasting a full five minutes. From three and a half months to four months increase the training sessions to two a day and make each session from five to ten minutes long. When the dog is four to five months old give two sessions a day, every day, and work from ten to fifteen minutes a session. In the course of the fifteen-minute sessions it is advisable to break the session up with several one-minute rests (and include rest time as part of the fifteen minutes).

A *five-to-ten-month-old puppy.* The full obedience course can be given in six weeks for a puppy in this age category. Begin with at least two training sessions every day, seven days a week, and make each session last between fifteen and twenty minutes. As the dog becomes seven or eight months old and if the training is still in progress, work him for two or three sessions a day, each session lasting a full twenty minutes. When the dog is working a full twenty minutes it is important to give him several rest periods. Work him five minutes and rest him for two minutes, repeating this regimen throughout the twenty-minute session.

A *young dog, ten months or over.* The course will take five weeks, six weeks at the most. Work the dog twice a day, thirty minutes each session, seven days a week. Give the dog two five-minute rest periods during each session. Work him ten minutes and rest him five minutes. His rest time should count as part of the thirty-minute session.

WHO TRAINS THE DOG

It is important that the same person teach the fundamentals of each command. However, it is not necessary for the same person to conduct each and every training session. It is very often not feasible for one person to devote all the time required to complete every session, every day of this obedience course. Once the basic technique of a command has been taught, other members of the family may conduct the sessions involving the repetition of the teaching process. The course does not have to be one person's complete responsibility. Many of the repetition sessions can be conducted during the course of a normal day's activities. For example, once the dog has been taught the fundamentals of "Sit" and "Stay" it is acceptable to practice the command during those times when you actually want the dog to sit or stay. This happens during dinnertime, when people come into the home, while watching television, etc. By utilizing the training sessions in everyday living you will reinforce the commands that the dog has been taught and save valuable time and energy. If the dog must go out for his walk then take advantage of that time to practice the "Heel," "Sit," "Stay," etc.

The length of time it will take a dog to complete this training course will be determined by the temperament of the dog inasmuch as it applies to his ability and willingness to be trained. In Chapter 4 ("Testing: One, Two, Three") you will be shown how to determine the behavioral temperament of your dog. Once his temperament has been established you will be greatly aided in the administering of the course.

THE TRAINING ENVIRONMENT

The first "teaching sessions" of every new command should not be a family affair. With a younger puppy, training should start indoors, in a quiet room with no distractions. Only one person may train the dog. As the dog progresses in his lessons you may allow more distractions to appear as a way of intensifying the learning process. *Once the dog gets his permanent shots (usually at twelve weeks) he may be taken outside for practice sessions and new commands.*

End every lesson with a happy fanfare. Hopefully this will make the dog look forward to the next time you train him. Complete the lesson when the dog performs properly so that you may end it with great praise.

Because a younger puppy is more easily distracted it is to be expected that his training will take longer. This especially applies to the command "Heel." It is the very nature of being a puppy for him to be curious and excited by every new experience, and certainly going outside will represent an entirely new world of experience. He is always going to be distracted and do not mistake his natural *puppyness* for an unwillingness to respond to you. Do not expect from a twelve-week-old puppy the same response you would get from a six-month-old dog. This is why it takes a young puppy twelve weeks to train while some dogs at six or eight months will learn everything in five lessons. It is a scientific fact, however, that a puppy trained at eight weeks of age will be a better-trained dog all his life than one trained at an older age. The reason is quite logical. You will *not* have had five or six months in which to make the kind of mistakes that permanently alter the dog's temperament. Remember the findings of Clarence J. Pfaffenberger, *"No matter how good his inherited character traits, if they are not given a chance of expression during this period* [the first sixteen weeks] *he will never be as good a dog as he could have been."* (Emphasis added.)

3

INSIGHTS

THE PROBLEMS

If happiness is a warm puppy then certainly reality is a wet one. Your new puppy loves you and everything about you, including your socks, your garbage bag, your eyeglasses, your towels, your hand-crocheted tea cozy, and your *TV Guide*. His slurping tongue is always a raspy shock when it scrapes against your mouth after cleaning God-knows-what with it. When you lift him up without looking at him some form of moisture is sure to get on your hands and one learns not to ask questions. Like a heartless lab technician, he is compelled to draw at least two drops of blood from your big toe when you least expect it. His baby teeth are like tiny sewing needles and razor sharp. But the little guy is absolutely certain that you enjoy all this and will only love him all the more for it. After all, you did pick him from all the rest, didn't you? And don't small puppies run giant households and all the people in them? They certainly do, for a while.

But nagging feelings of uncertainty quickly grow to the proportions of regret, misery, and free-floating anger after several days of full-fledged puppy ownership. This is almost always true for those who are experiencing for the first time the realities of taking in a cuddly creature that lives by its own rules. It is a rude shock to discover that Snoopy really is a comic strip and that one Collie does not a Lassie make. If little boys are made of frogs and snails and puppy-dog tails you ought to get a load of what's inside a little dog. They think they are little angels who can do no wrong. All they have to do is look at you with those soulful eyes as they cock their heads to one side and silently demand your love. They don't pay the slightest attention to your suppressed and growing frustration.

Let us attempt to describe this new puppy of yours. He jumps on people every chance he gets. He roams all over your furniture. Your hands are prime nipping targets. He spreads the garbage bag out like a new jigsaw puzzle. Grabs your food when he can. Begs at the table. Mouths. Growls. Talks back. Barks. Pulls hard on the leash. Urinates everywhere. Defecates on the floor and tries to cover it up with the carpet. And then really endears himself to you by howling and whining all night. Believe it or not, none of this is cause for despair. As George Bernard Shaw said, "The frontier [separating heaven from hell] is only the difference between two ways of looking at things."

This beastly behavior from your puppy or young dog is most certainly unpleasant and not the reward you expected for giving him a home. However, these things all indicate that your dog is a healthy, normal creature and will, with a bit of luck and training, grow into a mature and loving pet. If these characteristics are not present, then chances are he will grow into something less than desirable. All normal puppies are subject to bursts of energy, play, and misplaced body functions. They have various needs, drives, instincts, and emotions. A puppy should be curious and outgoing. His energetic desire for play indicates that his body and mind are growing and learning. It also indicates an ability to adjust to his new environment while learning to live with mankind. One should be concerned if the young creature is shy, immobile, and uninterested in food, mischief, and play. If you have a normal puppy as defined above, then the problem is really how to make the animal behave himself so that one can live in the same house with him. Although his annoying habits are signs of normal behavior they can become serious if not corrected at an early age. Cute puppy annoyances grow into serious dog problems later. What's cute now will be seriously destructive and frustrating after the dog has matured.

What we are trying to do is make every owner a dog psychologist in addition to being his or her own dog trainer. The emphasis is on diagnosis of each problem so that preventive measures can be taken rather than futile punishments administered. Positive solutions rather than negative ones. Many dog problems can be solved by rearranging the environmental factors rather than correcting the dog. These insights are based on the assumption that your puppy is a normal, outgoing animal rather than one with genetic problems or psychological maladjustments hopelessly far gone in time and intensity.

By learning these insights and developing those of your own you will be able to prepare yourself to solve problems before they even happen. With this technique you'll never fall out of puppy love.

THE SOLUTIONS

Whining at night. Put yourself in the puppy's place. It's his first week in a totally strange environment. He does not have the security of his mother or litter companions. He has never slept alone before in his young life. The darkness is frightening without the body warmth of his fellow creatures. He becomes anxious and tense and so he cries out in the night. New owners tend to fear that something is wrong with the dog or that he is simply poorly behaved. The mistake usually made is to yell at the little dog and threaten him with hands poised for smacking. Some people even hit the little tyke. Imagine a very small child away from home for the first time in his life, in the hospital or at summer camp. Think of your horror and outrage if the nurse or counselor hit him for crying after the lights went out. You'd think the camp was Oliver Twist's workhouse. If someone yelled at you for being lonely it certainly wouldn't solve your problem.

To help the puppy, put a radio on (soft music), and perhaps put something warm and comfortable like a blanket or hot-water bottle next to the dog. (Wrap the hot-water bottle in a towel.) Another possibility is a ticking alarm clock. Leave the light on. Give him some rawhide toys for chewing (except ones that represent an actual object that he might munch on later). Any one or all of these things will help both of you get a good night's sleep.

Nipping and chewing. Next to housebreaking, this is the main reason that people get rid of their dogs. The owner finds that he has been bitten on the fingers or that the little dog has chewed up something valuable. The owner's reaction is to punish the dog with a smack or worse. Of course the dog hasn't the slightest idea why he's been hit and learns nothing except to fear the owner's hands. One day, the dog has had it with being hit and goes on the offensive and bites back with a vengeance. Scratch one dog from a happy home.

Most puppies nip and chew because they are teething just like a human baby. One must discover the cause of a problem and work toward a solution in the most specific sense. No punishment in the world can stop the pain a puppy experiences from teething. Most nipping and chewing problems begin in puppyhood and continue into maturity where they develop into real trouble for both owner and dog. Now, if your baby cried because his gums hurt, you wouldn't yank his leash or knee him in the chest or smack him on the snout. You'd probably hold him, take a teething ring out of the refrigerator, and give it to him. You might even massage his gums with whiskey or paregoric. The same approach applies to a puppy. Let him chew on an ice cube; or soak a washcloth in water and freeze it, giving it to him afterward. The coldness will numb his gums and ease his pain. Think of how many times you'd never have to say "No" or "Bad dog." Easing the puppy's pain will lessen his desire to chew and help to avoid a bad adult habit.

Housebreaking. (See chapters 6 and 7.) This is the least pleasant aspect of owning a dog and the one most difficult for owners to learn to cope with. Without discussing the specifics of housebreaking and paper-training techniques we offer some insights on the problem. To begin with, there is a great difference between housebreaking and paper-training and that difference should be understood. *A dog is housebroken when he has been trained to relieve himself outdoors, at a time most convenient for his owner.* A dog is *paper-trained when he performs his bodily functions over newspaper in a designated area inside the owner's house or apartment.* It is important for the owner to decide early in the dog's life whether he is to be housebroken or paper-trained. To start the dog on papers and then switch to the outdoors is confusing for most dogs and invites accidents. It is only the occasional dog that can make the changeover with any great success.

The following information applies whether you decide to housebreak or paper-train. There are five key points involved in controlling your dog's bodily functions: (1) Correcting the dog. (2) Feeding-and-walking (or papering) schedule. (3) Proper diet. (4) Eliminating the odors from his accidents. (5) Confinement to one area. These factors are dealt with in their specific sense in chapters 6 and 7.

There are several factors that impede the success of a housebreaking or paper-training program if not understood and looked after. The sudden switching of dog foods will cause most dogs to suffer from a temporary case of diarrhea, which prevents the animal from controlling his bowel movements. It is best to decide on one kind of food and use it consistently. If you decide to change food it is best to mix both the old and the new food together and gradually increase the amount of the new food while decreasing the old. If you feed the dog all meat it will be too rich and also cause a loose stool, not to mention a possibly unbalanced diet. It is desirable to consult a veterinarian for the dietary requirements of each individual animal.

Do not change the dog's feeding times, especially during the housebreaking or paper-training period. Try to conform to a consistent schedule. It takes from six to eight hours for food to pass through the animal's stomach and this is an important factor in his walking or papering schedule. Some dogs are on self-feeding programs and those owners who adhere to such programs should try to determine the approximate times that the dog usually ingests food and schedule the walks and paperings accordingly.

Do not feed the dog from the table. It helps create the problem of begging, for one thing. Human food is often too spicy for dogs and upsets them. Most important, however, from the point of view of housebreaking, it disrupts the feeding schedule.

Before beginning housebreaking or paper-training, be sure the dog does not suffer from poor health in general and from internal parasites in particular. By this we refer to the various kinds of worms that often invade the dog's intestinal tract. There are roundworms (*Toxocara canis*), hookworms, whipworms, tapeworms, esophageal worms, and flukes. Any one of these or a combination of several will contribute significantly to a dog's inability to be housebroken or paper-trained. The dog simply has no control over his body functions in these situations. Professional medical treatment is absolutely imperative for the sake of the animal's health. Consult a veterinarian immediately. Although there are many and varied symptoms resulting from each respective parasite, certainly a rundown physical condition, prolonged diarrhea, listlessness, poor appetite, dull or shedding fur are strong signs and justify a visit to a veterinarian.

Chewing problems. Chewing problems start out small and end up big. If a puppy begins his chewing career by gnawing small holes in socks, you can be sure that he will be eating entire sofas by the time he matures. This habit most often begins when the owner allows the puppy to munch on old shoes, socks, plastic or rubber toys. It doesn't begin to get serious until the dog grows to maturity. Too often the dog chews destructively when the owner is not at home.

One should never tie the dog down and leave him alone. He is going to attempt to chew his way out. More harm is done, psychologically, by tying a dog down than by giving him some sense of freedom. It can lead to shyness or aggressiveness. It is also a bad practice to lock a dog up in a tiny room by closing the door. He may try to chew his way out. Dogs have been known to chew large holes in doors in order to gain an escape route. *The key is never to allow the dog to feel that he is trapped. This is a fundamental need of all dogs.* If you want to confine a dog use a gate or some other barrier that he can see through. If he can see his way out he will not necessarily feel the need to escape (unless he becomes very frightened).

One of the most obvious reasons for a dog's chewing habit is hunger. Be certain that you are feeding the animal the proper quantity of food for his size and bodily requirements. Here again, consult a veterinarian. It is also important to discourage the dog from nipping. If you allow him to nip at your fingers it is a simple carryover to the furniture.

Provide the animal with his own chew toys but make certain that they are made of rawhide or some other digestible material. However, do not give him a chew toy that is shaped like any identifiable object in your home. Avoid rawhide toys that look like shoes, cigars, pipes, etc. A proper chew toy may also help relieve a dog's boredom when left alone. So will a radio that is turned on.

Spitefulness. This is a subject that many dog owners feel very strongly about and it may be hard to win them over to the position of the authors. Spitefulness is a human behavior trait that people ascribe to dogs when, in fact, it is much too complex an emotion or thought process for them. Much destructive behavior from dogs is attributed to spite. How many owners have you heard say that their dog didn't greet them at the door because he had done something wrong out of spite or anger for having been left alone too long or because of some other alleged transgression by the guilt-ridden owner? This misconception is most strongly felt when the owner comes home to find that the dog has defecated on the bed, the rug, the laundry bag, or has simply chewed the house apart. It whimpers, its ears are down, or it's hiding under the bed.

However a dog misbehaves the reason is usually improper discipline, training, or correction. The reason dogs appear to know that they've done something wrong is that they associate your arrival with some form of punishment or scolding. After the animal's first encounter with your wrath he will always be apprehensive for the first few seconds of your arrival. It is true that dogs sometimes know they have violated their training but only after the fact. It is not spite work.

If the dog is a puppy he should be confined to one area when left alone. His area should be large enough so that it cannot be misconstrued as punishment. Do not give him the run of the house. If you do he will only get into trouble which you might interpret as spite because he didn't want to be left alone. This is nonsense. Most problems that are attributed to spite have to do with poor housebreaking, or none at all. The solution lies in reinforcement of the dog's housebreaking. If the dog has never been housebroken now is the time to start. If he has already been housebroken but is continually having relapses, go over the techniques as outlined in Chapter 6 and begin again. It is the only way to work. Dogs are not spiteful.

Jumping on people. This is one of those problems that need never have started. Who can resist the lovable puppy who crawls all over your lap in order to lick your face? He is sweet and charming. However, it is like teaching the dog to jump on people. Once he has been allowed this behavior as a pup he will continue to do it as he grows into a mature dog. Do not encourage the dog to sit on your lap, especially if you are sitting on the furniture. If you want the dog to express his love for you, sit on the floor and let him crawl, climb, and lick to his heart's content. Now, if you want the dog to climb all over you then you must allow him to do it on everyone. You cannot have it both ways. He cannot distinguish who he is allowed to jump on and who he is not allowed to jump on. Consistency is the only way to get the proper results.

This also applies to jumping on furniture. It is best to start out by not allowing the dog up on the couch so that the habit never gets started. Jumping up on the furniture, by the way, can contribute to the expensive habit of his chewing it or defecating on it.

Taking food from the table. Begging. Both of these problems are begun in much the same manner. The dog learns from his experience. If he is fed from the table (it always seems so cute), he's going to be at the table all the time looking for handouts until the day he dies. It's much more irritating (not to mention expensive) when he steals food off the table the minute your back is turned. Owners do not realize that they are the culprits in most of these problems. The misconduct begins because the dogs are encouraged, no, *taught* how to behave badly.

Never feed the dog from the table to begin with and chances are that the habit will never start. If you insist on giving the dog your table scraps (after his housebreaking training is over, of course), then take the food from your plate and put it in his. Do this away from the dining table. Let the dog eat in his own area only. Stealing food from the table grows out of begging at the table or improper diet. If the dog is truly hungry and not being fed enough he is going to steal your food.

Mouthing. This is when the dog constantly puts his mouth on your hand, your arm, your leg, or anything that belongs to you. There are many owners who think nothing of this and are not annoyed. For others it is disgusting and obnoxious, especially if you are the proud owner of a drooler (dogs that have Basset hound, St. Bernard, et al. in their genealogy).

Mouthing quite often begins when the man of the house plays roughly with the dog or puppy by baiting him with an arm or an old sock and plays tug-of-war. Although it may be good for the male image to roughhouse with the dog in this manner, it helps to develop a bad habit in the dog. Look for the man who names his dog Devil, Killer, Spike, Satan, Warlord, or Fang and you will find a dog who has been taught to mouth as a puppy or young dog. Show us a dog named Irving and we'll show you a dog that has not been taught to mouth.

This tug-of-war game can help develop aggressive characteristics that will be serious when the dog is older. The Doberman, Shepherd, and Terrier mixes are especially susceptible to aggressive games that start out with mouthing. The rule is simple. Do not put your hand or arm in the mouth of a puppy or young dog.

Eating his own stool (coprophagy). Here is an appetite-killer if ever there was one. It's also a conversation stopper if this unattractive habit takes place in front of friends or neighbors. If your dog indulges in this bit of indelicate behavior he is not only lacking in *savoir-faire* he's not much of an epicure, either.

This is definitely one of those habits that punishment cannot change. It is more sensible to attempt to find out what causes the dog to do it and try to change those factors at the root of the trouble. There are several possibilities causing the animal to behave this way. It can develop from continuous confinement and boredom. The dog might have adopted the habit if he has lived in a kennel longer than most dogs or if he has been left alone by his owner for great lengths of time. Puppies from retrieving-breed mixes would instinctively carry the stools around in their mouths. According to Dr. R. W. Kirk of the New York State Veterinary College, Cornell University, as quoted by the Gaines Dog Research Center, nutritional deficiency may play a part to the extent that puppies that have the habit are almost always infested with intestinal parasites. He states: "The vice of coprophagy appears to be most prevalent among hunting and working breeds."

Sometimes there is something lacking in the diet. There have been reports that the addition of salt, tomato juice, or sauerkraut juice to the dog's food, along with corrective measures, has helped to reduce or eliminate the habit. Diet in and of itself is not usually a factor unless, of course, the dog is simply underfed. There are commercial products that some veterinarians recommend that alter the taste of the feces and discourage the animal.

Obviously, the best cures are: Get a puppy that has not spent too long a period in a kennel existence; do not leave the dog alone for long periods of time; keep the yard and home meticulously clean of dog feces; give the dog plenty of exercise, play, and other forms of attention. A self-feeding, dry dog-food program is a good corrective measure. This will assure the dog of all the nutrition he requires and may check the problem. If you can catch the dog in the act you can correct him by saying "No" in a very firm voice and shaking a "throw-can" (see chapter 5).

Barking. Most dog owners never know they have a barking problem until they are accosted by an angry neighbor or a toothy landlord with an eviction notice in his hand. The reason, of course, is that the dog doesn't usually do his stuff until his master leaves the house. And who can blame that neighbor? The constant bark or whine or howl of a dog can drive one mad, especially if one isn't so keen on dogs to begin with. It's always a good idea to assume that a neighbor who does not own a dog is not exactly in love with them. This should be a guide to responsible dog ownership in terms of consideration for fellow human beings. A barking dog is a great nuisance and a guaranteed way of creating disharmony in your neighborhood.

There are many reasons why a dog barks. The most obvious one is simply that the dog has been left alone and is crying for the return of his master. Often a change of environment will create the problem, especially moving from a private house to an apartment, or the problem will develop with a change of owner. A nervous temperament often manifests itself by constant barking. Outside noises caused by strangers or moving vehicles will make a dog bark.

The way to work through the problem is to discover the cause, if you can. For example, a dog-owning couple moved from a private house to a two-family duplex. Their dog became a chronic barker every time he was left alone, something he had never done before they moved. It seemed that the couple felt that the dog would chew up the furniture if allowed the run of the house and consequently he was placed in the small hallway outside the entrance to their apartment. They had put themselves in a poor situation. In order to cope with the chewing problem they had created a barking problem. With the help of a professional trainer they solved their barking problem by ending the chewing situation. Once the dog stopped chewing up the furniture he was allowed inside the apartment and was never heard from again.

4

TESTING: ONE, TWO, THREE

*(How to Determine Your Dog's
Temperament)*

TESTING FOR DOG BEHAVIOR is not like testing for human psychology.
If you place a Rorschach ink blot test on the floor, in front of your dog
he will lift his hind leg and begin his paper training. To him, free
association means a leap onto your lap. Imagine a dog applying for
work and being asked to lie down on a couch by an industrial
psychologist, who suspiciously arches one eyebrow and asks, "Now
then, Mr. . . ah . . . Spot. How do you feel about dogs with pedigrees?
Do you like females? Have you ever been a bed-wetter? Do you bark
in your sleep? Actually, the employer wasn't really looking for a
mongrel. We'll let you know." Does it all sound painfully familiar?
Fortunately, most mutts get the job by virtue of a black spot over one
eye and a left ear that won't stand up. But understanding as much as
possible about the dog's personality is important if training is going
to be pleasant and effective. Testing for temperament is easy and
painless. Nobody loses. After all, the dog already has the job.

WHY THESE TESTS ARE IMPORTANT

The principles of dog training are very similar from trainer to
trainer even though each has his own variation. It is only in the
application of those principles that training varies from dog to dog.

For example, one would not use excessive authority on a nervous dog that flinched every time he saw a human hand coming toward him. Nor would one be permissive with a stubborn dog that knew how to bully his owner. Every dog has his own personality and behavior characteristics and these are the factors that determine how each aspect of obedience training should be applied.

The professional trainer's work is made much easier when he deals with a purebred dog, simply because he knows a great deal about the characteristics of that or any other breed. Weimaraners tend to be stubborn, Dobermans can be nervous or shy, Poodles are alert and responsive, etc. But what does the trainer do when asked to train a mongrel whose genes have been tangled around like a backed-up fishing line? If he's any kind of a pro he tests the dog for temperament before he even decides to accept the animal as a pupil. It is rare that a dog cannot be trained or, at the least, improved. However, it is necessary to understand the dog's personality traits and then be able to adjust the training techniques to the needs of the individual animal. These are the reasons that make this chapter the most important in the book.

WHAT IS TEMPERAMENT?

After an exhaustive search it has been impossible to find a scientific definition for the word *temperament* as it has been applied to dogs over the years. The derivation of the word is from the Latin *temperamentum*, which means "due measure or proportion," or a man's physical balance. The modern definition takes in a man's mental as well as physical characteristics as they relate to each other in proper harmony; hence, one's temperament refers to one's manner of thinking, behaving, or reacting.

Medieval physiology had a great hand in influencing the idea of temperament. Archaic medical beliefs defined the human body as containing four fluids—blood, phlegm, black bile, and yellow bile. These fluids were referred to as humors. Until the sixteenth century medical practitioners considered each fluid or humor to have a direct bearing on one of the four basic temperaments. The sanguine humor (blood) indicated a buoyant personality. The phlegmatic humor (phlegm) represented a sluggish disposition. The choleric humor (yellow bile) meant that one was hot-tempered. The melancholic humor (black bile) lent itself to depression, gloom, or dejection. It was believed that variations in a man's temperament indicated a fluid (or humor) imbalance. Once this theory was discarded the word *temperament* bounced around until it finally came to mean one's mental disposition (usually in the negative sense, i.e., The opera star was too *temperamental*).

It is extremely difficult to determine when the word was first used in relation to dogs and in what sense. Because Elizabethan references to dogs were hostile and unflattering it is possible that the negative connotations of *temperament* joined with the common literary attitude toward dogs ("Take heed of younder dog! Look, when he fawns, he bites"—*Richard III*). The other aspect of the word's definition, mixture and balance, may explain its long association with dogs when considering the dog fancier's obsession with genetics. *Temperament* is one of those words that we think we understand until we are called upon to define it. This is especially true when dealing with a dog's temperament.

To avoid confusion we are going to use the word in a very specific sense and, for the purposes of obedience training, ask you to accept our narrow definition. *Temperament* refers to a given dog's mental and emotional condition.

We have divided the various temperaments into six categories: nervous, shy, stubborn, sedate, aggressive, and responsive. Based on firsthand experience with thousands of dogs, these categories cover all behavioral characteristics in dogs *as they apply to obedience training*.

ABOUT TESTING FOR TEMPERAMENT

In order to help you determine your dog's temperament we offer a series of tests and observations for you to make as they apply to each of the six behavior categories. These tests and observations are for dogs up to ten years old. The ideal testing age is from seven to twelve weeks. The animal must be living with the owner in his home when the tests are administered.

For our purposes the words *temperament, personality,* and *behavior* are interchangeable. Two factors determine a dog's temperament: The first is the genetic factor and the second is environment. Because we are training mongrels there is little or nothing that one can say or do on the subject of genetic influence. Environment is quite another matter. In other words, how many mistakes has the owner made in shaping the dog's permanent behavior and how long has he had the opportunity to keep compounding those mistakes? It is rare that a dog is to blame for his own bad behavior. One must investigate the dog's home environment to understand why he does what he does, especially if his behavior is intolerable. A dog's poor behavior is too often attributed to stubbornness, stupidity, or spitefulness when, in fact, he is simply untrained. Some dogs are more intelligent than others. Some have brain tumors. Some are retarded. But there is no such thing as a dumb dog. So-called dumb dogs have either been abused or ignored or inadequately trained.

With obedience training an eight-week-old puppy can be mentally and emotionally shaped to the desire of its owner. A three-month-old puppy can be corrected and made to adjust his behavior to his home environment. An older dog can only be trained. His bad behavior characteristics can be controlled through obedience training but not permanently altered. An older dog that is nervous or shy will always be that way but, through training, will not be shy or nervous with his owner. Training is not a behavior cure-all. It only allows for behavioral compromise so that the dog can be a domesticated pet affording his owner many satisfying years of fruitful companionship.

It is recommended that chapters 9, 10, and 11 be read before conducting the temperament tests. Chapter 9 teaches the method of communicating with the dog through the technique known as the "Corrective Jerk." This procedure is utilized throughout the various tests and is essential for successfully completing them. Chapter 10 teaches the command "Sit," which is useful in the following procedures. Chapter 11 pertains to the command "Heel" and is incorporated in several tests. It is not important that these commands be learned to perfection. A casual familiarity with them will suffice for the purposes of this chapter. However, the Corrective Jerk, "Sit," and "Heel" must be learned thoroughly as the reader comes to them in the proper chapter sequence.

Once the tests have been administered and the temperament of your dog has been determined, you are as equipped as any pro to teach your dog obedience training that is tailor-made for his needs.

THE TESTS

THE NERVOUS DOG

Observations. A nervous dog never seems relaxed. He paces back and forth, sometimes in never-ending patterns. He may constantly follow you from room to room in a manner that indicates insecurity rather than playfulness. The dog is afraid to be without his master or mistress. His breathing and panting may be heavy. His constant movement has little to do with exercise. Sometimes his breathing sounds like he is having a heart attack. He may whine excessively when left alone or he might even bark loudly. The nervous dog never seems happy and barks at the slightest intrusion. He barks at the most inobtrusive noises and also at the sound of anybody coming near his domicile. This may happen whether the owner is home or not. The nervous dog is sometimes subject to sudden bursts of energy that will have him tearing around the house in an insane manner.

In some extreme cases the dog will develop a peculiar, glassy look in his eyes. It's hard to describe this look. He may look half-crazed or as if he is not focusing on anything in particular but rather is lost in thought. The dog is constantly on the move and will not obey any commands no matter how many corrections are administered.

A nervous dog will wet on the floor at the slightest change in the room. Many puppies wet because they've either drunk too much water or are very excited. The nervous dog wets because he is afraid—of punishments or of everyday events. This could be due to the temperament of his progenitors but is more likely because of his environment. Does there seem to be a nervous pitch in the dog's voice? Does his barking sound different from other dogs?

Tests for nervousness. Pick up the dog. Does he yelp and scream as though he were being hurt even though he isn't? How does he react? If he squirms and struggles to get free in a sudden panic it is a sign of nervousness.

Take the dog outside on a collar and leash. Walk the dog in the "Heel" position. He will probably run ahead. Give him a Corrective Jerk and say "No" in a firm tone of voice. Does he refuse to respond to the jerk? If he pulls harder as you jerk harder and starts yelping and fighting it is an indication of nervousness. Of course this applies more to older dogs than to young puppies.

How does the dog respond outdoors? Is he always looking around as if in danger? Does everything scare him? Do moderate noises frighten him? Does he shiver? When taken outside, especially in the city, a nervous dog never is relaxed enough to enjoy the new sensations and sights. It is hard to get him to walk by your side ("Heel"). He is always ahead of you or in back of you. He may cower against a wall or even grasp your leg with his front paws. This applies to puppies as well as older dogs. Sometimes a puppy won't walk at all. It is very common for a puppy not to walk when first taken outdoors. But if he resists with his front paws dug into the ground and yelps in fear it is probably because of a nervous temperament. This is especially true if the puppy or dog's yelp sounds as though you are hurting him when you know you're not.

Put the dog on a leash and see how he responds to walking with you. If he runs or acts terrified or stops dead in his tracks it may be due to a nervous temperament. He may also fight you, or leap in the air and do anything to get off the leash. This may even be nervousness mixed with aggressiveness (nervous-aggressive dog).

A nervous dog is often a chewer and will cause thousands of

dollars' worth of destruction in an apartment or home when left alone or not closely supervised.

When isolating these characteristics from the many, many positive traits of any dog the problems seem worse than they really are and, worst of all, they appear insurmountable. This is definitely not true. A nervous dog is eminently trainable. He requires more patience from his owner than usual. He needs more understanding and kindness than most dogs. The nervous dog should be trained by one member of the family in a quiet area with no distractions or elements that will frighten him. A dog of this temperament can be a good and loving pet. He simply has problems that must be dealt with before they cause other more serious problems.

THE SHY DOG

Observations. The difference between shyness and nervousness is the difference between being totally frightened and merely timid. It is, however, more than simply a matter of the degree of fear. In human beings shyness indicates a quality of personal insecurity and an inability to meet new people and situations in the most direct manner. Shy people need more time than other types to face the realities of change. They are extremely cautious, withdrawn in nature, easily embarrassed, awkward in the presence of others, and, most important of all, lack self-confidence. Any one or all of these qualities can apply to a shy dog.

The shy dog can almost always be found hiding under a table, a chair, or a bed. He doesn't greet people when they come into the house. He is afraid of noises and runs away when you pet him. If you accidentally drop something he will jump with fear or run away. When you put a leash on the dog his ears go down and he cowers with a drooping head. The expression on his face indicates that he is being hurt. As soon as you let this dog off the leash he will run under a chair or a table or a bed and not come out. Some shy dogs are perfectly well adjusted with their owners but will run behind their leg when a stranger comes into his house.

Tests for shyness. Use a throw-can filled with pennies (see Chapter 5). Shake the can just hard enough to make a noise without striking a chord of terror in the dog. If he runs away or hides under a table he is quite likely a shy dog.

Using a high tone of voice (as though speaking to a human infant), call the dog to you and give him an excessive amount of praise. See if he'll respond. If he comes to you reluctantly, he may be shy but somewhat responsive. Not coming to you at all is a symptom of shyness.

Have people the dog doesn't know come to your home. Notice how he responds to them. Does he run away? Does he back up and bark? Does he talk back to them? Does he hide between your legs? Does he run under the table and bark? These are all signs of shyness.

Put the dog on a leash and take him outside. How does he respond? If he refuses to walk it's a sure sign of shyness. Does he constantly entwine the leash around your legs? Is he afraid to venture out and explore new sights and sounds? Does he only want the comfort of your arms? If so, the dog is shy.

Raise your voice to the dog (without sounding hysterical). Do his ears go back? Does he lie down on his back in a submissive manner? He is probably shy if the answer is yes to these questions.

A shy dog can be responsive if he is given gentle care and much loving. Do not use the word "No" to excess and refrain from harshness or too much authority. If you do this the dog will at least learn to be responsive to the family. The key to handling and training a shy dog is patience and gentleness. He is scared and the only way to bring him out is to avoid harsh tones of voice or scare tactics of any kind. Be generous with your love and kindness. Sometimes it is necessary to gently coax the animal into obeying a command during the teaching process.

Once the animal has matured it is almost impossible for him to be anything but a shy dog. However, if you learn to cope with his shyness he will relate to "his family" in a fairly responsive way. What is more important is that his shyness not be allowed to worsen and develop into nervousness or aggressiveness. Obedience training will help to prevent this from happening.

THE STUBBORN DOG

Observations. Stubbornness in dogs is characterized by an unwillingness to obey commands or respond to corrections. A stubborn dog will sometimes growl in a menacing tone when his owner attempts to discipline him. A variation is when the animal talks back by barking or yipping after you have given a command. Stubborn dogs stand their ground in the face of punishment, threats, pleading, and all manner of persuasion.

Tests for stubbornness. If the animal tends to jump on people, set up a situation for him to do that. Place his leash and collar on him and have someone walk in. If he jumps on the person, administer the Corrective Jerk. If it takes many firm jerks to stop him from jumping, the dog is probably stubborn in temperament. Take note if the dog tries to stop you from jerking him by putting one paw on the leash or if he tries to stop the jerk by mouthing the leash and then growling at it. These, too, are indications of stubbornness.

Test the dog outside. Using the leash and collar, walk the dog in the "Heel" position. If he runs to the end of the leash give him a Corrective Jerk, say "No" in a firm voice, turn to the right, and walk in the opposite direction. If the dog gives you a fight, if he growls, if he bites the leash, if he puts his paws on the leash and refuses to walk, if he behaves wildly, if he refuses to move at all, if he jumps in the air—he is a dog of stubborn temperament. When outdoors for his walk look for these other signs of stubbornness: forcing you to jerk him four or five times every time you attempt to walk in "Heel," fighting you every step of the way, wanting the praise you give but refusing to work for it.

Test him with food. Place the leash and collar on the dog. Give the dog some of his favorite food, preferably with a strong aroma such as raw meat. After he has had a taste, place the dog in the "Sit" position. Take some of the same food and put it on the floor approximately five feet away from him. Hold the dog close to you with the leash. The instant the dog goes for the food give him a Corrective Jerk and say "No" in a firm voice. If you have to jerk him many times before he stops going for the food, he is a stubborn dog.

He will keep going for that food no matter how many times you jerk him. Incidentally, give the dog praise every time you jerk him so that he doesn't think he is being punished. If the dog takes six or seven jerks to stop going for the food, then he is responsive *to you* but must be considered stubborn.

A stubborn dog can be very responsive but it takes harder work. The corrections must be firm as must the tone of your voice. The stubborn dog must be made to realize that you mean it when a command is given and that he must obey it. Constant repetition of the teaching process and firm corrections when he refuses to obey will bring the best results.

THE SEDATE DOG

Observations. Most sedate dogs are very large and may come from the giant breeds such as St. Bernards, Newfoundlands, Great Danes, or Great Pyrenees. Several of the medium-to-small breeds also tend to be sedate and strains of them will contribute to this temperament. The Basset Hound and English Setter are among these types.

Sedate dogs are sensitive and will recoil from harsh tones of voice or excessive authority. These dogs are affectionate but do not express their emotion with the same exuberance as most others. They are quite lovable but tend to be quiet, easygoing, and lethargic. They love to sleep a great part of the time. Sedate dogs are responsive but in a very quiet way. They do not have many of the normal problems associated with most puppies. They don't jump very much. They don't nip. They don't chew. They're not excessive barkers.

Testing for Sedateness. Place the leash and collar on the dog and take him outdoors. Walk the dog in the "Heel" position. He may lag a bit. The sedate dog will not lag in resistance to the command but rather because he walks more slowly than the average dog. Call the dog to you after placing him in the "Sit" position. A sedate dog will lope up to you at a very slow pace.

Sedate dogs will respond to their owners in training but in a slower rhythm than other dogs. They take longer to respond to the teaching process during obedience training, but patience, consistency, and repetition of the teaching techniques are all that are needed to train sedate dogs. Their slow learning progress must never be mistaken for stubbornness or lack of intelligence. A sedate dog can be just as willing to please as any other animal.

THE AGGRESSIVE DOG

Observations. Aggressiveness is often attributed to an animal that is healthy, exuberant, and eager to live his life to the fullest. That is not the kind of dog we mean when we refer to one possessed of an aggressive temperament (unless otherwise specified). In our frame of reference an aggressive dog's behavior ranges from the bully to the vicious biter. He demands total control over all situations and does almost everything necessary to get it. The aggressive dog growls, barks, bites, chases, and even pushes other living things, and that includes small children and other animals. This kind of dog is, in short, a troublemaker and a creator of unpleasant situations either for the mailman, the neighbors, the meter reader, or his own family. If the dog is a puppy much of his bad behavior can be dealt with quite simply. Here, the Corrective Jerk works very well. But if the animal is adult he may not be capable of change. It is advised that professional help be sought for the fully grown aggressive dog.

The tone of a dog's barking is often an indication that he is aggressive. It is not hard to discern a friendly or playful bark from one that is menacing. It is a sign of aggressiveness if the dog barks at you after you have given him a command or told him to do something.

Testing for aggressiveness. Place the leash and collar on the dog and administer a Corrective Jerk. If he jumps and growls at you or starts biting or tearing at the leash, he is manifesting signs of aggressiveness. If the dog in question is a puppy then this behavior will seem playful and even entertaining. When this same dog becomes eight months old or more this very same behavior becomes frightening and, perhaps, terrifying. It must be stopped at an early age.

When the dog gets jerked observe how long it takes him to stop what he is doing. Does he stop right away? If it is necessary to jerk the dog more than two or three times and at the same time he snaps at you, he is aggressive. Some aggressive dogs will respond properly but still can prove to be quite mean. Their proper responses may only be with their owner in certain situations not involving more than one person.

Test the dog while he is eating. Observe his behavior when you try to take his food away before he is finished. Does he growl, curl his lip, snarl, go after you? If he does these things, administer a Corrective Jerk and see if he keeps it up or if he stops immediately. An aggressive dog will not tolerate anyone's interfering with his feeding. But a dog that is not aggressive should allow his owner to take the food out of his mouth. Incidentally, it is possible to stop this behavior by giving the dog a Corrective Jerk every time he misbehaves. This should always be accompanied with a firm "No!" Set up the food situation several times a week and correct the dog every time he growls or curls his lip. He probably won't lose his aggressive temperament but at least he will not snarl at *you* anymore.

Another test involves the animal's tolerance for persons other than his family. Simulate a situation with a friend who is a stranger to the dog. Place leash and collar on the dog and have the friend ring the doorbell. Answer it and admit the person to your home. If the dog barks and jumps on the stranger give him a Corrective Jerk. If the dog responds to the correction but still indicates that he wants to go after the stranger, the dog has an aggressive temperament. The aggressive dog will obey your command but unwillingly and will keep staring down the stranger with growls and a strain at the leash. He may even growl at you after the jerk if he is very aggressive.

Test the animal with other dogs. Does your dog, even a young or small one, pick fights with other dogs? Most male dogs become fighters at an older age. But when a young dog or puppy fights it's a sign of an aggressive temperament. We refer to a dog that isn't playing or simply mouthing the other animal, but rather is attempting to bite the other dog as severely as possible. This is something important to look for. Simulate a situation with another male dog and observe your dog's reaction. If your dog does pick a fight, give him a Corrective Jerk and say "No" in a firm voice. If he responds unwillingly or goes so far as to turn on you, he is definitely an aggressive dog.

It should be clear now that aggressive behavior will be apparent in various degrees. When a dog is intensely aggressive, great care must be exercised in handling him. Some are very dangerous. On the other end of the scale an aggressive dog can be a friendly one and only aggressive in terms of being a bully or one that takes advantage of his master. A mildly aggressive dog is not dangerous nor does he present any great training problems.

THE RESPONSIVE DOG

Observations. Dogs with a responsive temperament are, in fact, the easiest to train. They offer the least amount of difficulty and do not require special instruction. The authors believe that the majority of mixed breeds and mongrels possess responsive temperaments. This belief is based on experience with hundreds of mongrel dogs. The authors also believe that responsiveness is only one aspect of an individual dog's personality and is not necessarily the most endearing one. Dog personalities mesh with the various needs of their respective masters and what is desirable for one owner can be undesirable for another. A shy or nervous dog needs a great deal of patience and loving and will fulfill paternal or maternal needs. An aggressive dog may, possibly, give a robust man that *macho* feeling he is looking for. In other words, there is a proper home for dogs of every temperament and the responsive dog is merely one type of many that are useful, loyal companions.

Testing for responsiveness. By making your voice sound like a whining puppy you can tell how responsive the dog is. If he stops whatever he is doing to listen to this sound it is a clear indication of responsiveness. Observe what the animal does when you drop your keys near him. Does he stand his ground or does he run away? A responsive dog will not back away even though he is startled by the noise. He may even examine the object and sniff it. That indicates a healthy curiosity.

Feed the dog some of his favorite food. Then put on his leash and collar and place more of the food on the floor. When he attempts to get it, administer a Corrective Jerk and a firm "No." A responsive dog will either stop going for the food right away or go for it one more time, certainly no more than that. If he's responsive he'll probably just look at you and will not go for the food until you tell him it's okay.

With the leash and collar still on the animal, place him in the "Sit" position. Holding the leash straight up, over the dog's head, walk completely around the dog. Allowing more and more leash to slip out of your hand walk around him in larger circles, going farther and farther away. If the dog has not moved, drop the leash and see if he'll stay in place. If he does, he has an extremely responsive temperament.

Another test has to do with the change in your vocal tone. Allow the dog to get involved in any simple activity. In a very firm tone of voice say "No." Does the dog stop what he is doing, prick up his ears, and look up at you? That is the sign of a responsive dog. Changing the tone of your voice, call the dog to you using his name mixed with praise. Does he come over to you right away? That, too, is a sign of responsiveness.

Test the dog for jumping on furniture and people. Place his leash and collar on him and wait until he actually jumps. Give him a Corrective Jerk and a firm "No." He is very responsive if he corrects himself after one jerk. Give him much praise after each correction so that he knows you are pleased.

While the leash and collar are still on the dog take him outdoors and begin to walk with him in the "Heel" position. Walk and turn, walk and turn. If the dog keeps looking to you for the next move, you can assume that he wants to please you. If his attitude seems to indicate "Show me and I'll do it," he is a very responsive dog and he will need no special training instructions beyond what is written in each teaching procedure.

HOW TO USE THESE TESTS

Quite clearly, these simple tests can give you a fair appraisal of your dog's temperament as it pertains to obedience training. You may have discovered that your dog's temperament falls into more than one category. For example, he may be nervous-aggressive, nervous-shy, etc. In each case one quality will dominate over the other and that is the one to compensate for in the training process.

In every teaching chapter you will find variations of the usual teaching methods that are required by dogs of certain temperaments. They are referred to as Temperament Tips and are placed near the end of each teaching chapter. With some techniques a shy or nervous dog must be handled differently from a responsive or stubborn one. *Follow the teaching instructions of every chapter except when special instructions are given for your dog's temperament.* In that way you will be applying the techniques according to the special needs of your dog. Once you have determined the temperament category of your dog, you may both begin the obedience course.

5

TOOLS OF THE TRADE

(Things You'll Need)

THE RIGHT EQUIPMENT MEANS...

Never having to apologize for hurting the dog after applying a twentieth-century training device that was adapted from a fourth-century torture chamber. There is nothing exotic or expensive or complicated about the few items of equipment that you will need to successfully implement this obedience course. Equipment means those practical tools that are necessary to train your dog.

FROM THE DOG'S POINT OF VIEW...

Looking up at the shelves of equipment that some retailers display will not strike the same note of joy in your dog as would a walk through a new car dealer's showroom by someone with $10,000 to spend. What a horror it is for a dog to watch his owner spend many dollars for any one of the hundreds of gadgets that are offered ostensibly for the purpose of training or controlling an animal. Battery-charged shockers of all sorts seem to be very much in vogue. It is true that animals can be taught to behave in a prescribed manner through the use of electric shocks but no one has ever established whether that technique has done permanent mental or emotional damage to the trainee. The use of electric "shock treatments" on human beings is becoming less and less respected in the psychiatric world, and it is hard to find a modern institution that subscribes to that form of therapy.

Because we are a consumer-oriented society we too often place heavy stress on the purchase of manufactured products to solve our simplest problems. This is certainly true in the case of dog-training equipment. The variety of pet products numbers in the thousands and each item vows to solve one of the many problems connected with dog ownership. Obedience training as offered in this book utilizes only a few inexpensive tools. The rest has to do with behavior, communication, and the development of the relationship between dog and master. These are things that cannot be bought like a blue-satin rhinestone cattle prod. Save your money and spend your time with the lovable creature that you have taken into your home.

In regard to rhinestone-studded leashes and collars, hand-knitted sweaters, bootees, earmuffs, tail gloves, and all the liquids and powders that are for sale, you are advised that none of them has a blessed thing to do with training. They are for the most part designed for decor and decorum. One might add that the decor is definitely for the gratification of the master and does nothing at all for the dog's sensibilities.

Before primping and playing doll house with your dog consider his size, coat length and type, other physical characteristics, and his utility. Dogs should be allowed to look dignified, too. The point is that equipment has only to do with those items that help obedience-train the animal. Among those items there are several things that *will not* be needed.

DO NOT BUY . . .

Chain-metal leashes. Believe it or not a chain-metal leash will break sooner than a leather one. Its principal disadvantage is that it gives no advance signs of wear before breaking. A leather leash begins to wear thin in one or more places and draws your attention before it snaps in two. One can see the stitching become undone. A chain-metal leash may break suddenly while you are outdoors walking the dog. The result may be fatal.

Extra-fat, arm-length leashes. These are made of very thick pieces of leather and cost a lot of money. Although many people consider them attractive and, perhaps, masculine, they are virtually useless for the purpose of obedience training (see Chapter Nine, "Dancing to a New Tune").

Leather collars. This type of equipment serves no purpose in basic obedience training. A leather collar may be useful after the training period when the dog has proved to be a totally responsive animal, but it does not allow the trainer to administer an effective Corrective Jerk (see Chapter 9) and therefore can actually hinder the training process. Unfortunately, if your dog has long, delicate fur it may be necessary to use one in order to avoid rubbing the fur away at the dog's neck. A metal choke collar, in this instance, will create a permanent bald ring.

A pronged metal collar. This is a form of choke collar that would be at home in any medieval dungeon. It has spikes or bent prongs on the underside that tighten around the animal's neck when its slip chain is pulled. The metal teeth grip the dog's throat when yanked and squeeze and pinch the animal, thus restricting his movement. If the dog moves he suffers pain or, at the very least, great discomfort. Many professional trainers use this equipment and claim that, if used with great caution, it is an effective teaching tool for extremely stubborn (and large) animals. It is never recommended for the amateur dog owner. This dangerous collar can inflict permanent damage while making the dog suffer unnecessarily.

Pain and fear inflicters. Cattle prods, rolled-up newspapers, riding crops, wooden pointers, willow reeds, and whistles are totally unnecessary. Electric-charge collars that work by remote control can become destructive instruments in the hands of the average dog owner. All electrical devices, both home-made and manufactured, are definitely *not* recommended.

TOOLS FOR THE NONVIOLENT TRAINER

A *metal choke collar.* Do not be misled by the ominous-sounding name assigned to this most important piece of equipment. The word *choke* does not really apply because the collar does not perform in that manner. The metal choke collar is a short length of chain made of chrome-plated steel. Its links are small and should be welded together for maximum strength. At each end of the choke collar is a large ring. By properly looping the chain through one of the large rings you form a slip knot that is wide enough to slide over the dog's head. Be certain the collar is on properly (see Figure 1). The clip of the leash attaches to the outstanding large ring so that both dog and trainer are ready for a workout. Like any slip knot the chain will tighten around the dog's neck when the leash is pulled gently (see Chapter 9). When this is done the dog experiences a mild sensation. If the word "No" always accompanies this mild sensation the dog will learn that he has not performed properly. Thus, the choke collar becomes an extremely important communicative tool.

The collar must be placed around the animal's neck properly so that the operation of the slip knot is smooth. When the chain is tightened around the dog's neck it must remain tight for only an instant and then slide smoothly to its loose, hanging state. This is important if the dog is to avoid any pain. *The choke collar is not recommended for puppies, small and fragile dogs, or dogs with long, silky fur.*

A *nylon choke collar.* The nylon collar is ideal for puppies and very fragile small dogs. It is also best to use it for dogs with long or silky fur. The metal choke collar can wear away long fur from the dog's neck and create a permanent bald ring. Small and fragile dogs can be injured if jerked too hard with a metal choke collar. The nylon choke collar is recommended if your dog is a mix from some of the smaller terrier breeds, spaniel breeds, and breeds with sensitive necks such as Greyhounds and Whippets. Occasionally, the nylon collar will stick when jerked on a long-haired dog. Always check it to be sure the dog is not injured or pained.

A *six-foot leash.* A six-foot leash is precisely what is needed in this

1

Figure 1. Here is the choke collar as it is worn by *Spaghetti*. It is correctly placed in photo (1) (left) and incorrectly in photo (2) (below). The chain must hang so that it releases instantly after pulling it.

2

obedience course. It will be used in almost every training command and allows for the exact distance in many of the teaching techniques. This length is especially important when teaching "Sit" and "Come When Called." A leash made of leather is what we recommend most but the olive-colored canvas training leash is adequate. Many professional trainers use the canvas but we have found the leather to be more durable. It also avoids hurting the dog's chest or your hand when administering the Corrective Jerk.

When purchasing a leather leash you will be confronted with a wide variety of widths to choose from. Naturally, a dog's size will determine how wide the leash should be. However, five-eighths of an inch is best for most dogs.

Fifty feet of clothesline. This equipment is used when teaching the dog "Come When Called" *off-leash* and "Sit-Stay." During the teaching process you will be required to extend the leash beyond the six-foot distance. At this point you will attach the clothesline to the dog's leather leash.

The throw-can. This item is definitely a homemade tool and costs next to nothing to make in terms of time or money. Drink the contents of a beer or soda can and wash it. After it has dried drop a handful of nails, metal washers, or coins into it and then tape it closed with friction or masking tape. When shaken hard the can makes a great racket. As a matter of fact it will sound like a party noisemaker.

The throw-can is almost never thrown and certainly not directly at the animal. Do not use this equipment on a nervous or shy dog. It is not meant to terrorize or hurt the dog in any way. The object of the throw-can is to get the dog's attention when he is doing something wrong. When the can is shaken, the owner accompanies the noise with a firm "No!" This demanding noise and the firm "No" constitute a correction. Eventually the dog will stop what he is doing when he hears the word "No" unaccompanied by the throw-can. When dealing with an exceptionally stubborn or oversized dog, you may throw the can for a more intense effect. But the can should be thrown behind your back or in a direction away from the dog. He must never be allowed to think that he is being punished, hit, or hollered at.

Remember, you are correcting the dog, not punishing him. This tool will be useful during the housebreaking or paper-training process and is also implemented when solving the usual puppy problems such as going into the garbage, jumping on the furniture, chewing, etc. It will prove to be invaluable.

A *throw-chain*. Take a small choke collar and tie one or two knots in it so that it is rolled into a ball shape. It then serves the same purpose as a throw-can. Its principal advantage is that it can be used outdoors when teaching the dog his various commands *off-leash*. It will travel a great deal farther when thrown than the can. Although this item is manufactured it is not available in the average pet-supply store. It is something sold exclusively to professional trainers. As with the throw-can, you are again cautioned that this tool is not meant to be used to punish the dog in any way. It is used for correcting the animal. A firm "No" must always accompany the chain when it is thrown and it must never be thrown directly at the dog.

6

THE SWEET SMELL
OF SUCCESS *(Housebreaking)*

HOUSEBREAKING MEANS . . .

The dog has been trained to eliminate outdoors through proper scheduling of his feeding time, good discipline, and a healthy diet. He is never allowed to relieve himself indoors under any circumstances.

FROM THE DOG'S POINT OF VIEW . . .

Throughout a dog's life nothing, save survival, is more important to him than his own stool. It is his only tangible evidence that he exists. It is his exclusively to give, to leave behind, to claim territory with, to express satisfaction, to express fear, to indicate illness. It reeks of his exclusive odor and cannot be mistaken for the property of another dog or animal. The paradox of a dog's relationship with his feces is that at the same time that he wants it to remain where he leaves it, he does not want it too close to his living quarters. Somewhere between where he sleeps and where you sleep is the ideal location. It is for these reasons that the animal cannot grasp his owner's hostile and sometimes violent behavior toward his fecal matter. If a dog were asked to have his portrait painted while standing next to his most prized possession, it would certainly have to be his own excreted links. Those who have raised children understand this point best. How many parents have been chagrined when their three-year-old daughter has come running into the living room, shouting for all the company to hear, "Mommy, I just made stinky!" The pride. The joy. This is also true of the existential dog, your dog.

Housebreaking a dog is of prime concern to most new dog owners because the idea of urine and defecation on the floor is obnoxious. It is also destructive to carpeting and other forms of expensive flooring. But it is more than that. It is an agony, a series of major frustrations for the average person. Unfortunately, the indelicacy of the subject is too embarrassing for some and they go about dealing with the problem much like that three-year-old ("Did Boris make a tinkle-stinky on the six-thousand-dollar Persian rug? Naughty, naughty"). Although Boris doesn't deserve a medal for emptying himself on the carpet, he can't really be blamed, either. What would tinkle-stinky mean to you? The other reaction to a dog's evacuation in the house is what we call the Hitlerian Earthquake. The instant the owner sees the nasty indiscretion on the floor he falls down in a paroxysm of hysterical anger and lunges at the dog with every arm and leg flailing in the air. A variation of this behavior is when the owner jackboots across the floor with a menacing goose-step, grabs the quivering animal, and attempts to immerse him in his own body waste. One can almost hear the snare drums and bugles.

The most important reason for a dog's failure is his owner's inability to communicate what he wants. Knowing what to teach the animal is a major part of it. Because the dog's survival depends on his relationship with his owner, he is always trying to please. This is a fact. The only problem is that it has never been clearly communicated to him what it is that pleases the owner. He has, in most cases, dealt exclusively with the owner's wrath. Tell a dog he's a good boy or that he looks pretty, in short, give him approval, and watch how excited he gets. Imagine how often he would be excited if he were doing the right things in your house and you told him so. This is the essence of obedience training. You teach the animal the proper way to behave. When he finally starts doing things according to your teaching, you praise him for it. He then begins to work for your praise because it makes him feel good. If he fails to perform according to your rules you "correct" him and then give him immediate praise so that he never feels you are angry. Punishment does little for the teaching process. As a matter of fact it prevents the dog from learning.

A dog is never partially housebroken. This fact was proved by the man whose dog never messed in the house. He always took him outside. Once, while walking his dog, he stopped for a few moments to chat with a friend. His partially housebroken dog discreetly squatted and dumped neatly on top of the man's shoes.

Have you ever heard a dog owner rationalize about his dog's lack of training? "Von Rhinelander is most certainly housebroken—he just can't resist making *wee-wee* on silk—or cotton—or wool . . ." If your dog is a fetishist, maybe his problem is simply that he hasn't been housebroken properly. Is he or isn't he?

Paper-training is not housebreaking. Do not confuse these two distinct methods. They represent different life-styles for the dog and each has its own demands and requirements. A housebroken dog never eliminates anywhere but outside the house in which he lives. If a dog is taught to use newspapers as a puppy and is then expected to learn to go outdoors he is bound to become confused and make mistakes throughout his life. In this situation the dog may never understand why he is being taken outside. He'll just sniff around and wait for you to take him indoors and back to his newspapers.

Many veterinarians suggest that a newly acquired puppy of eight to twelve weeks should not be taken outside because the animal is too young to have received all of his permanent shots. If this situation applies to you and you have decided that the dog is to be housebroken, here is a suggestion: Do not attempt to paper-train the dog. Select an area that is convenient for you and the dog and place several sheets of newspaper there. When the puppy is about to eliminate place him on the papers but do not scold him or correct him in any way. The same applies if he has an accident off the papers. Although it is a nuisance you will be rewarded for your patience once the housebreaking begins. Once the veterinarian says the puppy is allowed to be taken outside the newspapers should be removed completely and the housebreaking training should commence. This is very important if you do not want to confuse the animal.

The housebreaking technique that follows is probably the most humane as well as the most effective ever offered. It demands of the dog owner a certain amount of time and effort, patience, a total abstinence from violence or punishments (it makes the heart grow fonder), and an understanding that the dog's urine and defecation has a special meaning to him. Housebreaking is one of the key factors in maintaining a satisfying relationship between dog and owner. Too many dogs have been abandoned or given up for adoption (or execution) because of the owner's inability to solve this problem. Here then is an opportunity to help the dog keep his happy home without suffering the pains of failure.

HOW TO . . .

The problem with housebreaking is that it is always approached from a negative point of view. Many dog owners start this process with a sense of dread or disgust and wind up hating the poor dog for putting them through the so-called ordeal. Of course, it's not fair to the dog but, more importantly, it need not be so terrible a chore if the owner knows what he is doing. Information and a well-organized plan make housebreaking easy and afford one a sense of unique accomplishment. This technique is based on five elements: (1) Correcting the dog (punishment forbidden). (2) A feeding-and-walking schedule. (3) Proper diet. (4) Getting rid of the odor. (5) Confinement to one area.

The ideal time to housebreak a dog is as soon as he is brought into the home. This, however, depends on how quickly the animal gets his shots and whether the veterinarian says the dog may be taken outdoors. Puppies from eight weeks to ten years have been successfully housebroken with this method. It should be understood that a young puppy or dog will be more responsive to training than a six- or eight-year-old. The younger the dog is the easier it is going to be. But there is no rule that says you can't teach an old dog new tricks. Although it will take longer to housebreak an older dog, the method will work if the owner adheres to all the prescribed techniques.

If the animal has already been using newspapers for several months he will probably not defecate when taken outdoors. Many puppies are acquired at Christmastime and are not able to sustain the cold weather. Consequently, they have been using newspapers for the entire winter and are completely baffled when taken outdoors. The transition for this animal will be more difficult and will require persistence on the part of the owner.

While some dogs seem to have a natural instinct for being housebroken others take much longer. The training period for this technique may take between two and four weeks, depending on the age of the dog and his willingness to please. But no matter what the circumstances one should realize great progress in the first week of training. If there is no progress by the second week, it is possible that the animal is not well and should be taken to a veterinarian. If a dog has worms, as many puppies do, he will not be able to control his digestive system and housebreaking becomes virtually impossible until the condition is corrected.

Assuming the dog is allowed outdoors and is in good health, the following five elements must be scrupulously adhered to with no deviation. Each element is given in the best possible order to successfully housebreak your dog.

1. CORRECTING THE DOG

Among the many misconceptions of dog training, hitting the dog is the greatest. It is a mistake to think that the dog has learned something by being hit or yelled at or by having his nose rubbed in his own mess. The underlying philosophy of this method of housebreaking, indeed, this entire obedience course, is simply that the word *correction* must be substituted for the word *punishment*.

You can correct the dog only when you witness the mistake. The mental grasp of most dogs is extremely limited. Therefore, a dog cannot associate a smack on the rump with a mess on the floor if he transgressed before you arrived on the scene. Even a few minutes after he messed is enough time to make him stare dumbfounded and wonder why you are hollering. It confuses the dog. Punishment, even proper correction, effects very little after the fact. Spare yourself the energy and the dog the confusion. Correct the animal only when you catch him in the middle of his bad deed.

The correction itself. Assuming the dog is urinating or defecating indoors during the housebreaking period, and is doing it in front of you, there is only one way to respond. You must startle the dog so that he stops what he is doing and then run him outside to finish.

One must not holler, hit, or threaten the animal. Do not use rolled-up newspaper or pointed fingers to terrorize him. It is here that the throw-can comes into play (see Chapter 5).

Here is the proper sequence for correction: The animal transgresses. You shake the throw-can vigorously, making a loud racket and accompanying the noise with a firm "No!" The dog will look up at you. Moving quickly, place his leash and collar on and run him outside to finish what he started. Once he does, praise him lavishly. The net result is that you have stopped the dog from messing completely on the floor while *teaching* him where that process is to take place. *This is the only way the dog can be taught.*

Temperament tips: Be certain that the dog's temperament can tolerate a vigorous shaking of the throw-can. Using discretion is very important here because you can win the battle of housebreaking but lose the war of obedience training. A shy or nervous dog can become acutely disturbed by too intense a correction and may become aggressive as a result. The tone of your voice when saying "No" must also be modulated in this situation. The shy or nervous dog must be treated somewhat more gently than the rest. Stubborn, sedate, aggressive, and responsive dogs can tolerate a vigorous shaking of the can and a firm "No." With some stubborn dogs it may be necessary to actually throw the can instead of merely shaking it. Slam it to the floor in order to stop the dog from eliminating. It is essential that the can be thrown away from the dog (behind your back) so that he doesn't misconstrue it as an object of punishment.

The most important aspect of the correction is the word "No."

This must always be said when the can is shaken so that the dog will eventually respond to the word itself without any other sound or action. This corrective technique is one that teaches rather than terrorizes. It is designed to communicate to the dog that he is doing something wrong and the extra step of what he should be doing. The leash and collar are problematic. One must choose whether to let them remain on the animal most of the time so that he can be rushed outside with no delays or to have them standing by in a convenient place. Taking a dog outside in the middle of his digestive release requires that you have speed and agility.

2. FEEDING AND WALKING SCHEDULE

The following schedule must be strictly adhered to for the entire housebreaking-training period. Please take note that there are different schedules for dogs of different age ranges. The training period should last only between two and four weeks, the feeding and walking schedules should then be adjusted according to the needs of the dog and the convenience of the owner. As the dog gets older, change his schedule to the one that applies to his age range. You will find that in most cases the number of feeding times recommended per day is consistent with those suggested by professional dog people. Still, it is best to seek the advice of a veterinarian for the needs and requirements of your dog.

Schedule for Puppies Three to Six Months Old

7:00 A.M.—walk the dog.
8:00 A.M.—feed, water, and walk.
12:30 P.M.—feed, water, and walk.
4:30 P.M.—feed, water, and walk.
8:00 P.M.—water and walk.
11:00 P.M.—walk the dog.

Schedule for Six-to-Ten-Month-Old Dogs

7:00 A.M.—walk the dog.
7:30 A.M.—feed, water, and walk.

12:30 P.M.—water and walk.
4:30 P.M.—feed, water, and walk.
11:00 P.M.—walk the dog.

Schedule for Dogs Ten Months and Older

7:00 A.M.—walk the dog.
7:30 A.M.—feed, water, and walk.
12:30 P.M.—water and walk.
6:00 P.M.—water and walk.
11:00 P.M.—walk the dog.

(In some cases a veterinarian will require that a ten-month-old or older dog be fed twice a day. In that case add a feeding, watering, and walk at 4:30 P.M. and eliminate the 6:00 P.M. watering and walk. In that way the animal will have six and a half hours to eliminate his final meal before bedding down for the night.)

The success of this housebreaking method depends on absolute consistency. Feed, water, and walk your dog according to the schedule that applies to your dog. When feeding the dog allow him fifteen minutes to eat and then take it away no matter what is left in the bowl. Wait five minutes before giving him water. This will help avoid regurgitation. Provide him with all the water he wants before his walk. Do not feed the dog other than what he gets at the scheduled time. For puppies and young dogs water should be made available at all times. Ask your veterinarian about all matters pertaining to your dog's intake of food and water.

The more one regulates the time for food and water the closer one comes to scheduling the dog's digestive process. In cases where water must be provided at all times reduce the quantity and supplement the bowl with ten or fifteen ice cubes when leaving the house for several hours. This will reduce the animal's water intake but satisfy his thirst at the same time.

After feeding and watering the dog according to his schedule, take him out for his walk *immediately*. Allow him to pick a preferred spot to empty and praise him the minute he relieves himself. Return indoors the minute the dog is finished. You will be creating a conditioned reflex that will imprint itself on the dog's mind for the rest of his life. It will not be long before the dog understands why he is being taken outside. It is important that you not allow the dog to remain outdoors for exercise when he is being walked for housebreaking purposes. If you walk the dog for a long period of time either before or after his digestive release he will never fully understand the point of the walk. Walking for exercise should be eliminated during the housebreaking period. Give the animal a long play period indoors, instead.

Schedule for People Who Work (Any Age Dog)

7:00 A.M.—walk the dog.
7:30 A.M.—feed, water, and walk.
Home from work—walk the dog.
Immediately after walk—feed, water, and walk (again).
8:00 P.M.—water and walk.
11:00 P.M.—walk the dog.

Obviously, no young dog or puppy will be able to hold in his need to empty when first beginning this schedule. The solution is to confine the animal to an area, while you are at work, where he can urinate or defecate without causing damage to the house. Place newspapers over that entire area and never correct the dog for messing there. Take up the papers the minute you arrive home and allow the dog to run around the house *providing* you watch him for mistakes.

3. PROPER DIET

Many of the most complete scientific studies of small-animal nutrition have been made by the commercial dog-food manufacturers. The result has been the marketing of superior commercial dog food. The proper balance of vitamins, minerals, proteins, carbohydrates, and fats is essential to the well-being of your dog. These essentials can be obtained from a combination of meat (fresh or canned) and commercial dog meal. Some commercial foods contain all the essentials in one product. Whether you decide to buy commercial dog food; prepare it at home, supplementing it with vitamins; or buy prescription-type dog food, check with your veterinarian first.

Under no circumstances should leftovers from your dinner table constitute the dog's diet. For one thing, it encourages the dog to beg for food while you are eating. But, most important of all, there is no way to know for sure that the animal is getting all the nutrients he requires. If you plan to change the dog's diet as a result of what we have suggested, do not do it all at once. Over a four-day period add some of the new food to the old food, increasing the amount each time as you decrease the old food. A sudden change in diet very often upsets a dog's sensitive stomach and causes diarrhea.

Once you have settled on the proper diet for your dog do not vary from it. It will have a direct bearing on the success of the housebreaking. No food or doggie treats should be given to the dog between his feeding times. Avoid the temptation if you want this training to work. And, finally, allow the young puppy an extra walk if he consumes a large amount of water after a playful run around the house.

4. Getting Rid of the Odor

Most dogs return to the same area (sometimes the same spot) to urinate or defecate. The reason for this behavior is they are attracted to the smell that still lingers. All dogs have an unusually well-developed sense of smell and can call up from their memory as many as 10,000 different scents. You can wash the area in which they have made toilet accidents with detergent, bleach, ammonia, and all manner of room deodorizers and the dog will still be able to smell the spot on which he last urinated. He can smell it even if you cannot.

When you take your dog outdoors observe how he behaves before he empties. He will search and hunt with his nose to locate a place that is very specific to his sensibilities. What he is doing is claiming his territory or marking on top of another dog's claim. His claim or mark is made with his own urine or excretion. He will return again and again to the same location both indoors and out. It is important in housebreaking that his odors be obliterated from inside your house. This can only be accomplished with the use of an odor neutralizer.

There are several commercial preparations available in pharmacies and pet-supply outlets. One such product is called Nilodor. These neutralizers are not perfumes of any sort and come in concentrated form as a liquid. When used properly they can completely destroy the scent of the dog's waste material, so that he cannot discern it.

During the housebreaking period wash all areas in which the dog has messed with the odor neutralizer. Half-fill a pail with hot water and place ten or fifteen drops of the neutralizer in it. Mop all areas where the dog has messed. The dog will begin to mess indoors less frequently once his odors cease to exist in the house. This must be accomplished each and every time the dog has an accident.

5. CONFINEMENT TO ONE AREA

It is usually when you leave the house that the unhousebroken dog will do his worst, which is especially true if the dog has been punished for messing in front of you. The only answer to avoiding a ruined home is to confine the dog in an area that is least offensive to you when he has accidents. With the exception of very young puppies, most dogs will try to avoid messing in an area that is close to where they have to eat and sleep. Puppies have almost no control and will not be able to help themselves. The area of confinement should be where the dog eats and/or sleeps. The area should be provided with a folding gate rather than a closed door so the dog does not feel that he has been punished or banished from his home. In the case of small puppies a baby's playpen will do nicely. If the area is too small the dog will whimper or bark excessively and may even try to escape.

Under no circumstances should the dog be tied down with a rope, chain, or leash when you leave the house. Tying him down will have an adverse effect on the dog's temperament and will ruin your chances of housebreaking the animal.

When you come home release the dog from his confinement and *do not punish him if he has messed on the floor*. Remember, you can correct the dog only if you catch him doing it. Now that you are home again, allow the dog to run loose but keep a close watch over him. If he gets out of your sight and messes on the floor there is nothing you can do and you will have wasted one entire day of housebreaking training. Be in a position to correct the dog and run him outside the minute he starts to relieve himself.

RANDOM THOUGHTS ON HOUSEBREAKING.

Like people, no two dogs are alike and only the owner knows the dog completely. Therefore, when settling down to the routine of the feeding-and-walking schedule, take the dog's individual quirks into consideration. Some dogs do not empty for half an hour after they've been fed. In that case, delay the walk for that required amount of time. Some dogs empty shortly before they are fed. That, too, must be considered in determining the proper time for a walk. Be flexible and adjust the schedule according to the dog.

On very rare occasions one is faced with a dog that will not empty outdoors, which may be caused by early paper-training, age, or stubbornness. If after many days of scheduling and the other training techniques the dog still refuses to relieve himself outdoors, you may try utilizing a baby suppository just before taking him out. You are cautioned to use this method as a last resort and not to continue it for more than two days at the most. Consult your veterinarian about this. Feed and water the dog. Then insert a small baby suppository in the dog's anus. Take the animal outdoors immediately.

Never confine a dog in a closed-off bathroom. It is too small an area. The ideal locations would be a long hallway, a den, or any single room closed off by a see-through gate. Otherwise, you may resolve the housebreaking problem but start a chewing or barking problem. If the dog is nervous or very excitable, a larger area is suggested.

The common mutt is truly a remarkable creature. He has no papers from the American Kennel Club. He has no pedigree. And yet, just like the $1,000 purebred dog, he will dump all over your house if he isn't trained. All dogs are brothers under the skin.

The next page is meant to be cut out of the book so that it may be hung in a convenient spot during the housebreaking-training period. All you have to do is write in the dog's feeding and walking schedule so you or a member of the family can tend to the animal's needs without fail. You must also write in the dog's diet so there can be no mistakes there, either. This special cut-out sheet may prove to be invaluable.

Housebreaking Tearsheet

Remove this page from the book and post it in a conspicuous place.

Special Instructions and Reminders

Your dog should have all his shots before being allowed outdoors.

Do not confuse paper-training with housebreaking. Remove all newspapers.

All food is to be taken away from the dog after fifteen minutes.

No food or doggie treats between meals.

The dog may wet out of excitement or nervousness. This is not a mistake. Do not correct him.

NEVER HIT YOUR DOG

NEVER HOLLER AT YOUR DOG

NEVER PUNISH YOUR DOG

CONSULT YOUR VETERINARIAN

Feeding-and-Walking Schedule

Time	Activity (Feed, water, walk)	Food Amount	Type (per meal)
_____	_____	_____	Cereal or meal
_____	_____	_____	Canned or moist
_____	_____	_____	Vitamins
_____	_____	_____	Supplements
_____	_____	_____	Coat conditioner (oil or capsule)
_____	_____	_____	Other_____

7

YELLOW JOURNALISM

(Paper-training)

PAPER-TRAINING MEANS . . .

Your dog will eliminate his bodily wastes over newspapers that have been spread on the floor in a convenient location in your house. Once the dog has been trained in this manner he will not use the outdoors for this purpose.

FROM THE DOG'S POINT OF VIEW . . .

The disposable paper toilet is as close to you as your nearest newsstand. For a nominal price you not only receive the events of the day, you are given the world's least expensive throwaway canine commode. To the novice dog trainer, paper-training, as a way of life, brings new dimensions to such expressions as paperweight, wrapping paper, paperwork, and, alas, wallpaper. But despite the adjustments involved, paper-training is pleasant and convenient for most dogs and offers the dog owner an alternative to housebreaking.

Most dogs mark their territory with urine or feces, which explains why they prefer one spot in particular whenever they are taken outdoors to eliminate. But with the advent of scoop laws, motorized street cleaners, and irate non–dog owners, the territorial markings disappear much faster than ever before. The dog no sooner empties and turns around for a smell than it's gone. This is not a problem for the paper-trained dog. Although the solid and liquid material disappears the subtle but discernible scent remains (to his nose only) to reassure the animal that his home is indeed his territory.

It is also a fact that the paper-trained dog is never confronted by that angry segment of the population that resents his use of the streets for toilet purposes. The new owner also enjoys not being squeezed between that faction of citizens who believe they have no civic responsibilities in relation to their dogs and another group that would irresponsibly and cruelly force owners to give up their pets or endure undue hardships to keep them. Comfortably, almost heroically, squatting between these two extremes is the paper-trained dog.

It is by no means suggested here that all dogs should be paper-trained. Certainly very large dogs and older dogs would have a difficult time with this method. But when one considers the number of new puppies that are added to every city each year and that some percentage of them could be paper-trained, it becomes obvious that a substantial dent could be made in the problem. If the quantity of dog litter were reduced in the city streets, the specter of so-called scoop laws would fade and paper-training would transform extremists of every persuasion into paper tigers. If a dog were given his choice of facing the angry types on both sides of the question or using paper in the privacy of his home, he would certainly opt for the latter.

They like it. When a dog is a very young puppy he can be trained to behave as a perfectly domesticated pet. At this age paper-training can be introduced most successfully, assuming that the owner has, of course, chosen this method as a consistent life-style for the animal. The puppy, and most older dogs, appreciate the quick removal of body waste from the living area. The urine tends to be absorbed by the paper, which is, ultimately, removed in short order.

Do not use any of the paper-training techniques if you intend to housebreak the animal as soon as the veterinarian says he can go outdoors. You will only confuse the dog and possibly make him neurotic. He then will have one accident after another, for which you will probably punish him and, consequently, destroy his sweet temperament.

If your dog is too young to go outdoors and you plan to housebreak him, simply lay papers down and do not correct him if he fails to use them. Try to direct him to the papers and tolerate his accidents until he is old enough for the housebreaking techniques. In the case of an older dog you will have to exercise greater patience and possibly endure a longer training period. The changeover from housebreaking (or no training at all) to paper-training for a mature dog is difficult for both dog and master.

HOW TO . . .

As with a human baby, a dog's body waste must be removed (or at least dealt with) by the mature person in charge of the situation. It is no more or less repulsive than any other aspect of life. The major difference between a baby and a puppy is that the baby grows into a mature, self-sufficient being and the puppy always remains dependent on his owners. This is an important reality to face when deciding to acquire a dog. It is a minor liability when compared to the companionship, devotion, and utility one realizes from fifteen gratifying years with a dog.

The techniques of paper-training are based on six easy elements: (1) Papering the dog. (2) Correcting the dog. (3) Feeding-and-papering schedule. (4) Proper diet. (5) Getting rid of the odor. (6) Confinement to one area.

Once the choice has been made to paper-train the dog rather than housebreak him, the techniques may be utilized immediately no matter how young the puppy is. If, on the other hand, you are going to train a large male dog older than one or two, we offer this word of caution: It is possible that he will not be able to prevent himself from urinating on vertical surfaces such as the refrigerator or, perhaps, the walls. One should stay alert to this possibility and observe the dog's responses as training progresses. In the event that a large male dog instinctively lifts his hind leg to urinate, compensate for it by placing the newspapers closer to the center of the room. Keep him as far away from vertical objects as possible.

Paper-training may take from two to four weeks to complete but positive results should be noticeable within seven days. If there is no progress by the end of the first week, it is possible that the animal is infested with internal parasites. He should be taken to a veterinarian immediately. Almost every dog and puppy gets worms at some point in his life. One important symptom is an inability to control his digestive system, which, in effect, would make paper-training impossible until the condition is corrected. Once you are certain that the dog is in good health you must follow the six training elements with absolute consistency.

1. PAPERING THE DOG

This element is probably the most fundamental of all six and the most important. The entire paper-training technique hinges on this aspect. First, select a convenient location in your house where the dog may relieve himself without upsetting the family. This location must be where he will be confined when the family is not at home to watch him. In most instances it is the kitchen, basement, hallway, or bathroom.

Next accumulate as large a stack of newspapers as possible and a supply of large plastic trash bags. You are now ready to begin. Spread a three-to-five-sheet thickness of newspaper over the entire floor of the room. Do not leave one area uncovered by the papers. This is where the dog is to be taken when it is time for him to relieve himself. With the papers covering every spot on the floor it is impossible for him to make a mistake. *Every time the dog empties on the papers remove them, but save one sheet that is stained. This sheet should be placed underneath the fresh paper near the spot he soiled.* Although you will not be able to smell it, the scent will be attractive to the dog and draw him back to that spot when he's ready to empty again.

Allow the papers to remain on the floor twenty-four hours a day during the training period. Change them every time they become soiled. A puppy will relieve himself many times during the course of one day and that is to be expected. All dogs have certain signals that indicate they are going to urinate or defecate. By constant observation one can learn to recognize them and take the dog to the papers before it's too late. As the dog matures his need to empty occurs less frequently.

Continue this procedure for five days. At the end of that time begin reducing the area covered by the newspapers. Lay down less and less paper every day so that eventually you are using only that amount of paper the dog needs to relieve himself. It will soon become apparent that the dog has settled on one spot in the room as his favorite place. In a matter of days you will only have to put papers there. Some dogs confine themselves to one spot very early in the training. When they do, start reducing the papered area immediately. For the average dog the process should not take more than ten days.

Once the dog has been fully paper-trained it is only necessary to lay down the papers just before the dog is about to use them. This is optional. If the dog has responded perfectly to the training and his feeding schedule has been consistently established, he may be trusted to go to the papers at his discretion and you may leave them out for him all the time.

2. CORRECTING THE DOG

Throughout this obedience course you are urged never to punish your dog, never hit your dog, never holler at your dog. A correction is a technique of communicating to the animal that he has done something wrong. It must be followed immediately by one or two actions: Either teach the dog right then and there what he is supposed to do or praise him so that he does not think he has fallen into disfavor. Using fear or terrorizing the dog is counterproductive and actually impedes the learning process. It is also inhumane.

You can correct the dog only when you witness the mistake. It is useless to correct the animal unless you catch him in the middle of his incorrect behavior.

The proper correction. In paper-training, the proper correction is saying "No" in a very firm tone of voice and using the throw-can. Nothing else is required or desirable. Do not point your finger at the dog as if to say "Naughty, naughty." One's hands should be used only for things that will create pleasant associations for the dog. For instance, you feed the dog with your hands, examine him for medical reasons, express affection to him, and render hand signals for obedience commands. But if you smack the dog, hit him with a rolled-up newspaper, or point an accusing finger at him, he will always fear your hands.

When the animal makes the mistake of relieving himself in front of you in a nonpapered area, here is what to do: Immediately say "No" in a very firm voice. Reach for the throw-can and shake it vigorously, making a loud noise. The object is to startle the dog and impress upon him that his action displeases you. The next step is the most important. Immediately carry the dog to his papered area and let him finish there. Once he does, lavish him with praise. This is the teaching part of the training. You have stopped the dog from emptying where he should not and shown him where it is considered desirable. Because all dogs essentially want to please their masters, they will begin to work for praise by trying to do the right thing.

Temperament tips. In using the throw-can one must be cautious and consider the temperament of the animal. If the noise is too harsh or the correction too authoritative, dogs of certain temperaments can become disturbed and develop bad behavioral traits. A nervous dog can tolerate a normal shaking of the throw-can accompanied by a firm "No." But a dog with a nervous-shy temperament cannot tolerate the throw-can at all and you should use a soft tone of voice when saying "No." A nervous-aggressive dog is different. Here, you must shake the can very hard and accompany it with a loud "No." This kind of dog is usually very excited and requires a great effort to stop him once he has started.

For the shy dog do not use the throw-can and modulate your voice for a very soft "No." A stubborn dog requires a normal shaking of the can and a firm "No." The sedate dog should not be subjected to the throw-can and requires a firm but soft "No." Dogs that are aggressive should have the throw-can shaken vigorously with a loud "No." Dogs that have responsive temperaments should have the throw-can shaken vigorously at them but then only need a soft "No."

To reiterate what was said in Chapter 6, the most important aspect of the correction is the word "No." It must always be said when the can is shaken so the dog will eventually respond to the word itself without any other sound or action. This corrective technique is one that teaches rather than terrorizes. It is designed to communicate to the dog that he is doing something wrong. But remember, it has absolutely no value if the dog is not then taken to the proper place and shown where he can relieve himself.

3. Feeding-and-Papering Schedule

If the dog is fed in the same area or room where his papers are (as is so often the case), one merely takes away the food and water in order to give the dog the opportunity to empty himself. This is what is meant by the term "papering the dog." If the dog is fed in a room away from his papers, he is to be taken to his papers wherever it is indicated to him to be "papered." When the animal is being papered he should be confined in the paper area for not less than ten minutes or until he has relieved himself. His food must not be present and his water should be taken away temporarily. Once the dog has relieved himself, give him a great deal of praise and make a big fuss so that he knows that he has pleased you.

The schedules that follow must be adhered to if the paper-training is going to be successful. There are several schedules offered and they pertain to the age of your particular animal. Use the one that applies to your dog. These feeding-and-papering schedules are applicable for the duration of the training period only. Afterward, they can be adjusted according to your individual needs, the age of the dog, and the advice of your veterinarian as it pertains to your animal's nutritional requirements.

Schedule for Puppies Seven Weeks to Six Months Old

7:00 A.M.—paper the dog.

8:00 A.M.—feed, water, and paper.

12:30 P.M.—feed, water, and paper.

4:30 P.M.—feed, water, and paper.

8:00 P.M.—water and paper.

11:00 P.M.—paper the dog.

Schedule for Six-to-Ten-Month-Old Dogs

7:00 A.M.—paper the dog.

7:30 A.M.—feed, water, and paper.

12:30 P.M.—water and paper.

4:30 P.M.—feed, water, and paper.

11:00 P.M.—paper the dog.

Schedule for Dogs Ten Months and Older

7:00 A.M.—paper the dog.

7:30 A.M.—feed, water, and paper.

12:30 P.M.—water and paper.

6:00 P.M.—water and paper.

11:00 P.M.—paper the dog.

(In some cases a veterinarian will require that a ten-month-old or older dog be fed twice a day. In that case add a feeding, watering, and papering at 4:30 P.M. and eliminate the 6:00 P.M. watering and papering. In that way the animal will have six and a half hours to eliminate his final meal before bedding down for the night.)

The key word in paper-training is *consistency*. Once you start a feeding, watering, and papering schedule you must not vary from it if the training is to work. Allow the animal fifteen minutes to eat his food and then take it away no matter how much he may have left in the bowl. Wait five minutes and then allow him all the water he requires. By waiting the five minutes you may prevent a vigorous eater from regurgitating his meal. After the dog has been papered allow him to have all the water he wants and keep it available to him. During the training period do not allow the dog to have any food or treats between his feeding times. This is important if his body is going to be regulated. However, consult your veterinarian on all matters pertaining to your dog's nutritional needs.

Exercise. The fact that a dog is paper-trained does not mean he is never to be taken outdoors. All dogs need exercise and play and that is usually provided by a vigorous walk and/or run. Obviously, these walks must not interfere with the feeding-and-papering schedule. It is very easy to get the dog confused if he is taken outside before he has had the opportunity to empty on the papers. Once he is taken outdoors there is no way to prevent him from marking the territory with urine. Young puppies are usually not allowed outdoors until they have received their final shots. It is absolutely essential to confer with your veterinarian on this matter.

Schedule for People Who Work (Any Age Dog)
7:00 A.M.—paper the dog.
7:30 A.M.—feed, water, and paper.
Home from work—paper the dog.
Immediately after papering—feed, water, and paper (again).
8:00 P.M.—water and paper.
11:00 P.M.—paper the dog.

4. PROPER DIET

It is now accepted by many persons in the dog world that a dog's nutritional requirements are as influential to his physical and psychological well-being as genetic stability and environmental influences. The proper balance of vitamins, minerals, proteins, carbohydrates and fats is essential to the growth and development of the animal and an intelligent and consistent diet is of immeasurable importance. This is especially true of training in general and paper-training in particular. These essentials can be obtained from a combination of meat (fresh or canned) and commercial dog meal. There are many commercial dog foods on the market and most of them are sufficient to meet your dog's requirements. If there is the slightest doubt about what to feed your dog we suggest you consult your veterinarian.

In order to promote the proper rate of growth and development and maintain the best possible state of health it is recommended that the dog *not* be fed a diet of leftovers from your dinner table. A dinner of leftovers, no matter how large a quantity, does not guarantee with any certainty that the dog is getting all the nutrition he needs. Also, feeding a dog from the table actually teaches him the annoying habit of begging for food.

If you have not been feeding the animal properly and have decided to change his diet, do not make the change suddenly. A dog's stomach is quite sensitive to dietary change and he will develop diarrhea quite easily. Over a four-day period add some of the new food to the old food, increasing the amount each time as you decrease the old food. This will help his stomach make a smooth adjustment to the change.

5. Getting Rid Of The Odor

Upon careful observation you will notice how most dogs insist on emptying themselves in the same area and, quite often, on the same spot that they soiled before. This is due to the animal's incredible sense of smell. He can discern his and any other animal's excretory odor no matter how faded and undetectable to humans. Because he combines his sense of smell with an instinct to claim territory with urine or feces, it becomes clear why a dog keeps messing up the same spots in the house he shares with his master. In order to discourage the desire to return to the same soiled spots in the house, the owner must obliterate those odors that remain. They must be neutralized each and every time the animal has an accident in the house.

Unfortunately, the more obvious commercial products will not eliminate the scent of your dog's waste material. He can smell it for many months after you've washed it with detergents, bleaches, ammonia, and room deodorizers of every description. None of these products is strong enough to remove the subtle odor that remains. It can only be accomplished with the use of an odor neutralizer. There are several preparations available in drugstores and pet stores. One such product is called Nilodor. These products do not attempt to cover up the scent with a strong perfume that smells sweeter. In a chemical action this liquid concentrate interacts with the original odor and neutralizes it completely so the dog cannot go back to it. This is very important in paper-training. Once the dog has had an accident, been corrected, and shown where to go, he is thoroughly discouraged from returning to the scene of the crime.

Each and every time the animal soils an area of the house that is not his paper area, it must be cleaned with the odor neutralizer. Half-fill a pail with hot water and place ten or fifteen drops of the odor neutralizer in it. Mop all areas where the dog has messed. You will soon notice that the dog has fewer and fewer accidents in the house. He will want to return to the familiar area that you have chosen because it is the only place that has his scent. Praise him every time he uses the papering area. Let him know he has pleased you.

6. Confinement to One Area

It is sheer insanity to allow an untrained dog to have absolute freedom of the house when no one is there to watch him. During the paper-training period the puppy or dog must always be watched so that he can be corrected in the middle of an accident. But when the owner must leave the animal alone he must be confined. If not, he is quite capable of doing hundreds or even thousands of dollars' worth of damage. Aside from any chewing destruction the dog will surely defecate and urinate all over the house. There are several reasons why he will wait for you to leave (none having to do with spite). First, the dog may be frightened or nervous when left alone. Many dogs express fear and terror by defecating. A constantly ringing telephone, unanswered, may startle him. A stranger at the door can have the same effect. Second, he may get bored and relieve himself simply to make life a little more interesting. Third, he may decide to mark off his territory. Fourth, if he's been hit in the past for relieving himself in front of you he is certainly going to wait for you to leave the house before he does what gives him so much pleasure. And fifth, he simply cannot hold it in. This is probably the most common reason. For these reasons the dog must be confined to one area where it is acceptable for him to soil the papered floor.

This area should be where he is usually papered. With the exception of very young puppies, most dogs will try to avoid messing in an area that is close to where they have to eat and sleep. Puppies do not have very much control over their digestive systems and will have to empty themselves wherever they happen to be at the time of need. Assuming the dog is papered where he eats and sleeps he will not relieve himself too often while you are away and he is alone. This will help teach him to control his body and wait until you are there to change his papers.

It is suggested that this area of confinement be large enough so the dog does not feel he is being punished when placed there. It should not be closed off by a solid door. If the area is too small or the doorway blocked off the dog will whine, howl, or bark excessively and you will come home to some angry neighbors or a belligerent landlord. Install an inexpensive folding gate in the doorway so the dog can see into the next room without getting out. In the case of a small puppy, tack chicken wire to the bottom of the gate so he cannot wriggle through the openings.

Under no circumstances should the dog be tied down with a rope, chain, or leash when you leave the house. This will have an adverse effect on the dog's temperament and will ruin your chances of paper-training the animal.

Upon your arrival allow the dog to leave the papering area; clean up any soiled papers (saving one); and praise the dog for having used the papers. Your homecoming should be a source of pleasure for both you and the dog. Next, allow him to run loose in the house and watch him for accidents. Do not punish him if he messes on the floor. Correct him if you catch him in the act. If he gets out of your sight and messes on the floor there is nothing you can do and you will have wasted one entire day of paper-training. (For additional useful information read Chapter 6, "Random Thoughts on Housebreaking.)

The next page is meant to be cut out of the book so that it may be hung in a convenient place during the paper-training period. All you have to do is write in the dog's feeding-and-papering schedule so you or a member of the family can tend to the animal's needs without fail. You must also write in the dog's diet so there can be no mistakes there, either. This special cut-out sheet may prove to be invaluable.

Paper-Training Tearsheet

Remove this page from the book and post it in a conspicuous place.

Special Instructions and Reminders
Do not confuse paper-training with housebreaking.
All food is to be taken away from the dog after fifteen minutes so that he may be papered.
No food or doggie treats between meals.
The dog may wet out of excitement or nervousness. This is not a mistake. Do not correct him.

NEVER HIT YOUR DOG

NEVER HOLLER AT YOUR DOG

NEVER PUNISH YOUR DOG

CONSULT YOUR VETERINARIAN

Feeding-and-Papering Schedule

Time	Activity (Feed, water, paper)	Food Amount	Type (per meal)
_____	_____	_____	Cereal or meal
_____	_____	_____	Canned or moist
_____	_____	_____	Vitamins
_____	_____	_____	Supplements
_____	_____	_____	Coat conditioner (oil or capsule)
_____	_____	_____	Other _____

cut along dotted line with razor blade or scissors

8

VERBAL TOOLS *(No/Okay)*

The dog must stop whatever he is doing when this verbal command is given. "No" is most commonly used as a correction and is never said during the teaching process. A dog can never be corrected for something he has not been taught.

FROM THE DOG'S POINT OF VIEW . . .

Although negative words and sounds are not terrific they are a blessing when they are concisely used in a crisp, clear manner—in other words, if the owner knows what he wants the dog to do and understands how to communicate what he wants. The average dog must try to sort out ten to fifteen different exclamatory commands that essentially are meant to mean one thing but really mean ten other actions. For example, "Get out of there," "Cut it out," "Behave," "Stop," "Don't," "Rondo, heel," "EEyaah," are all meant to get the dog away from the garbage can. It is impossible under those circumstances for the dog to have the faintest idea what the owner really means. It can only lead to a dog's confusion and insecurity.

It is unreasonable to expect a dog to refrain from dumping in your shoes if you suddenly yell, "Sit!" Think about that for a minute.

"Sit" is a command. "No" is a correction and is meant to stop the dog from whatever action he has started. "Sit," "Stay," "Down," "Heel," "Come," are all commands that involve movement to some degree. The dog cannot stop one action and begin another simply because you have commanded him to do so. He must be stopped from his first action and then commanded to start another. "No" will accomplish that.

Get to "No" your dog properly. There are two incorrect directions to go with this word, anger or timidity. The dog slops through a freshly paved, cement sidewalk and then runs into the house toward the new wall-to-wall carpeting. You are about to go into cardiac arrest and scream at the top of your lungs "No!" The veins in your neck bulge and your face whitens from the lack of blood. Of course the dog does stop short of the carpet but has also released a terror-ridden, soft stool on the hallway floor. He has also been traumatized for life and will fear going into your living room for any reason. In this case "No" has become a four-letter word and destroys the dog's confidence in his own home.

The other side of this coin can be worse. Your six-pound Poodle mix, Brunhilde, comes running into the living room in front of the members of the church bazaar committee with a sack of dirty laundry in her mouth. While your guests start counting the rosebuds on the wallpaper you whisper to dear Brunhilde, "Noooo." She drops the sack and starts removing the contents one item at a time. You whisper "No" once more and then begin chasing her, knocking over teacups and cake plates on stiffened laps and kneecaps. And then, of course, your solution is to relocate the meeting on the patio. Two negative factors are at work in this situation: the inhibition to discipline your dog in front of strangers and, much worse, the fear of alienating the animal's affection. Neither factor is rational or desirable. It is a fact that most dictators throughout history have been small, and the same applies in the pet-owner situation. Many a dog has ruled a large household with all its members bowing to all demands made by the little cur. This can be very bad for the dog because sooner or later some member of the household will decide it's time to get rid of the tyrant. When this happens the dog's future is in grave jeopardy. He may be abandoned, given to an unkind owner, or sent to his death in a government shelter. A firm "No" at the right time can avoid all this.

Name-dropping. When a dog hears his own name he should be wagging his tail and getting ready for something pleasant. This is extremely important in the command "Come When Called." It would take an idiot to respond to someone who was going to hit him or reprimand him. It is for this reason that one never uses the dog's name with the word "No." The animal should never have the opportunity to associate its name with something negative.

All commands that involve forward motion are called *action commands.* "Heel" and "Come When Called" are action commands. The dog's name is always prefixed to the action command so that he knows he is going to move forward whenever he hears it. For example, "Muffin, [pause] Heel." At the sound of "Muffin" the dog is alerted to the idea of forward movement. This association is formed by repetition of the command in the teaching process. Because of this use of the dog's name it is imperative that his name never be used with the word "No." There is no word more negative or authoritative than "No." It should only be used when it is necessary or desirable to stop the dog in the middle of bad behavior. At that point it is unnecessary to use the animal's name.

Repetition is the mother of hysteria. When it is necessary to correct the dog do not use the verbal tool "No" more than once. It seems inevitable that emotions flare up quickly when the dog compounds his mistake by refusing to respond to a correction after he has already misbehaved. Such a flareup is damaging to both dog and master. There is nothing more humorous to a stranger than witnessing a dog owner go berserk on a city street as he screams at his dog, "No! No! No! No!!! " Once the owner realizes that people are watching he either walks away having let the dog go uncorrected or he hits the animal. Both negative results are the product of frustration and rage.

It is not outrageous to say that the dog will shortly behave like his owner and will also make public displays of hysteria. Certainly genetic heritage is not the only cause of nervous-tempered dogs.

Skittish, neurotic dogs are very often made that way by their owners' behavior. The dog would much rather that you make your correction in a no-nonsense manner indicating that you mean what you say and that he had better respond properly. Naturally, this is achieved through proper teaching but here the owner's training is of equal importance. All dogs respond to the human voice according to its tone. If you say "No" in a very mild tone of voice it is not really clear to the animal that he is supposed to stop what he is doing. If you exert too much force or a note of emotion (anger, frustration, rage) the dog will be too frightened or confused to do anything but cower or attack or defecate or any combination of the three. You must learn to talk to your dog in a cool, professional manner so that he never feels you are angry with him but, at the same time, understands that he must obey.

Dog talk. When it is time to give the animal his due praise for obeying a command properly it should be done in a high-pitched tone of voice. Because dogs are babies that never grow up they may be spoken to in that manner. They love it. When delivering a command your voice must be calm, resonant and authoritative in a friendly way. Now, when correcting the dog with the word "No" the voice must sound different. Shouting is no good. Draw in a deep breath of air and allow it to expand the muscles of the stomach. As you allow the air to escape say the word "No" so that it rides out with the released breath. You will notice a deeper, firmer tone of voice than you have ever produced and it will not reflect any unnecessary harshness or emotional overtones. This is the proper way to say "No" and expect to command the dog's attention. Once the difference between praise and correction is clear to the animal you will realize results that you never imagined possible. All dogs will work hard to get praise if it is given with enthusiasm and affection. If the praise is withheld and substituted by the firm tone of correction, he knows he must cease and desist his wrong behavior. Success depends on the owner's clarity and consistency.

HOW TO . . .

Deliver a firm and resonant "No" whenever the dog is behaving in an undesirable manner. Bear in mind that "No" is a correction meant only to stop the immediate action. Immediately following the correction give the dog praise for having obeyed you. Then you may command the dog to "Sit," "Stay," "Come," "Down," etc. Don't forget to praise the dog each and every time he obeys your commands.

You should never have to correct the dog by saying "No" more than once. If the animal doesn't obey the first time then it is possible that your voice is not firm enough. "No" is also used in conjunction with the Corrective Jerk (Chapter 9) and with the throw-can (Chapter 5). The throw-can is principally used in housebreaking (Chapter 6) and paper-training (Chapter 7). The use of "No" as a correction is explained fully in each of the above chapters and will help reinforce this verbal tool.

Temperament tips. For dogs of a nervous temperament use a firm "No." For nervous-shy dogs use a very gentle "No." A very loud "No" is required for nervous-aggressive dogs. A shy dog demands a very gentle "No." The stubborn-tempered dog will require a very firm "No." Use a gentle "No" for the sedate dog. Aggressive dogs must get a very loud "No." Dogs that are considered responsive must be dealt with firmly as indicated in the beginning of the chapter.

"OKAY" MEANS . . .

One of two things. First, it is a release from training or walking in "Heel." It is also used as a prefix to the dog's name when utilizing the command "Come When Called."

FROM THE DOG'S POINT OF VIEW . . .

Just as the animal must know when a command is being given he must also be able to distinguish when the discipline is over. The verbal tool "Okay" must be positive in sound and represent something very pleasant to the dog. If it does not it is absolutely useless. If the word is said with irritation or any tone other than an exuberant one it will defeat its purpose. It is also important that you do not confuse the dog by using the word for any but its expressed purpose.

HOW TO . . .

A verbal tool to release the dog from training or the command "Heel." After a training session the animal should be told that the learning is over for the day and told in as pleasant a tone as possible. "Okay" can be said in a high-pitched voice or simply in a cheerful, happy tone. The higher you pitch your voice (as if talking to a baby) the more excited and happy the dog will be. *"Okay,* Thelma; that's all," should make the animal feel deliriously happy and bring a jumping, running response.

When walking in the "Heel" position the dog is on the owner's left side with his head near the master's left thigh. There is approximately two feet of leash extended from the owner's hand to the dog's collar. This is explained fully in Chapter 11. The limited length of leash greatly restricts the dog's freedom as both walk down the street. This is exactly as it should be even when the animal is being taken out for housebreaking reasons. It is not until the animal reaches the area where he usually empties that he is released from the restricted length of leash. This release is accomplished with the verbal tool "Okay."

Assuming you are walking on the sidewalk you say "Okay" in a very happy voice and allow the dog to have all the leash he needs or wants (never release the leash entirely). The dog should go directly on the street, off the sidewalk itself. If he does not, it is easy to guide him there. After several repetitions the dog will know what to do without your help. This release will become extremely important to the dog and he will look to you in anticipation, waiting for permission to empty himself at the correct location. At that point, we suggest that you stand back.

"Okay" when calling the dog. One is never 100 percent sure that the dog will come when he is called if he is off-leash and outdoors. This requires long and arduous training and is very difficult for dogs one year or older. If the dog does not associate the use of his name with something pleasant (your praise) he may not come to you. It is here that "Okay" becomes very useful. When the dog is farther than twenty yards away you will have to raise your voice to call him, which could be misconstrued by the dog as a reprimand. To counter that effect you call the dog by prefixing his name with "Okay," and use a very exuberant sound. It should be, *"Okay,* Taylor, come!" If you say it properly, the dog will be reassured that you are not calling him in order to administer punishment. "Okay" is one of the more positive-sounding words in the language and is very difficult to say in anything but a cheerful tone of voice. Because your dog has learned to work for your praise he will come to you when you call him because he knows you will give him approval and playful attention."Okay" will always be a joyous-sounding word throughout the dog's life and will give the owner many rewards if he uses it correctly.

9

DANCING TO A NEW TUNE
(How to Use the Corrective Jerk)

THE CORRECTIVE JERK MEANS . . .

Snapping the leash quickly and firmly so that the dog understands he has not performed properly. It is almost always accompanied by the verbal correction "No." The leash is attached to the choke collar so the dog will feel a mild sensation when the jerk is executed properly.

FROM THE DOG'S POINT OF VIEW . . .

It doesn't hurt! Because very few dogs write, read, or speak English (or any other human language) it can be very difficult to communicate with them. This absence of meaningful communication between man and dog makes life unnecessarily hard for both. The dog wants very much to please his master and gain love and protection. But it is difficult for the animal if the master does not know how to communicate what he wants from the dog. The Corrective Jerk is one of the most useful means of coping with these problems.

It is a tool for communicating to the dog that he has done the wrong thing and must pay better attention. *It is the only way one can teach a dog obedience without abusing him.* There are two steps to training a dog. The first is to let him know what he has done wrong. The next is to teach him the proper way. Unfortunately, many people let the dog know of their displeasure by terrorizing him with punishments or threats of punishment and then let it go at that. The error is to assume that this is sufficient to get the animal to do what is expected. The Corrective Jerk tells the dog he has done wrong in a painless and nonabusive manner. When used skillfully, it also guides the dog through the teaching process and actually shows him the correct way of doing things. It is absolutely essential in this obedience course.

Imagine how grateful a dog will be to finally have found a line of communication that enables him to please his master. Do not misunderstand, it is not always fun and games for the animal when the Corrective Jerk is administered. Some resist it like a child being forced to do his homework or accept a vaccination. But the positive results cannot be questioned. The value of the Corrective Jerk cannot be overemphasized. It will be used over and over again in teaching every command in this course. Once the owner and the dog understand this communicative technique a mutual respect will develop and continue for the entire length of the relationship.

Past experience has made it clear that the dog does not like his first encounter with the Corrective Jerk. It is a surprise and a bit upsetting. Although the animal never feels pain he does experience a jarring sensation that is foreign. When the leash is jerked, the sound of a firm "No" accentuates the negative communiqué and the dog experiences the emotion of rejection. Eventually, the dog loses this sense of rejection because he has been praised after every Corrective Jerk. It then becomes more of a guidance tool. That is why it is absolutely essential that the dog be given great praise immediately following each and every Corrective Jerk. He must never be made to feel that he has been punished.

If given his choice a dog would rather not have a Corrective Jerk. What the dog does enjoy is that inarticulate pleasure when his master says, "That's a *good* boy. Nice fella." That comes after one really firm jerk has been administered so that the animal was able to

Figure 2. This is the proper step-by-step method for holding the leash with both hands. Holding the leash in this manner is important when administering the Corrective Jerk. It enables the trainer to effectively correct the dog without hurting him.

3

4

5

correct himself. A few firm corrections are much easier on him than many weak and ineffective ones. Gratuitous or excessive use of this technique will alter the dog's behavior negatively and make him fear it like a slap. One must use the Corrective Jerk with economy and only when it is necessary. If the word "No" is used with every jerk, the master will eventually be able to use the verbal correction exclusively. The dog's mind will have been conditioned to the master's corrections for his entire life and will always respond to them.

HOW TO . . .

Equipment. Two items are necessary to execute the Corrective Jerk. You will need a choke collar and a six-foot, leather leash. By stringing the metal links through one of the rings the collar forms a slip knot when placed around the dog's head. The leash clip is attached to the collar ring that dangles away from the dog's neck.

Position. Place the dog in the "Sit" position, on your left side. Both you and the dog should be facing the same direction.

Holding the leash properly (see Figure 2). Place the thumb of your right hand through the top of the loop of the leash. The lower part of the loop hangs down across your open palm. Next, grab the leash in the middle with your left hand and bring it to the palm of your right hand. Wrap it one time around the thumb of your right hand. The leash should now stretch from the dog's collar, across your knees, with a slight slack in it, leading upward into your right hand. The excess leash dangles by your right leg, forming a large loop. With your right hand held waist-high adjust the length of the leash so that there is no more than the width of your body (allowing for a slight slack, of course). Close the fingers of your right hand around the various strands of the leash that are within your grasp. Your closed fingers, palm facing upward, now have as firm a grip as possible.

You are now going to reinforce the grip with the other hand. With the left hand placed directly under the right hand, grasp the various strands of leash. The knuckles of the left hand should be facing upward so that each hand grips the leash in an opposite direction. You are now in a position to execute a very firm Corrective Jerk. In addition, you have absolute leash control of the dog's movements. It is almost impossible for the average dog to bolt from any adult, man or woman, with this grip.

Jerking the dog. The dog is in "Sit" by your left side. You are both facing the same direction. Both your hands are holding the leash as described above. Your hands are held slightly below your waist. Jerk the leash quickly toward your right side and return your hands to their original position immediately (Figure 3). When you jerk the leash the choke collar will tighten around the dog's neck and deliver a mild sensation. Return your hands to their original position instantly and the collar will automatically loosen, thus avoiding pain for the animal. Only your arms should move during the jerk and they should head sideways and slightly upward and back again like a spring. The action is Jerk and Release; Jerk and Release. The collar must tighten around the dog's neck no longer than a split second. This is very important.

With every Jerk and Release give the verbal correction "No!" If you consistently use the verbal correction with the Jerk and Release you will eventually not have to jerk the dog at all. A firm "No" will be all that is necessary to make any correction or stop the dog from misbehaving.

Praising the dog. Verbally praising the dog after each and every Jerk and Release must be considered an integral part of the Corrective Jerk. Praise cannot be emphasized enough. Such phrases as, "That's a *good* boy. Good fella. Atta boy," are the sort of praise that keep the dog's temperament even. It assures him that you are not angry with him and that love and approval are always there, providing he obeys properly. *Once you correct the dog you must automatically praise him whether he performs properly or not.* He must never misconstrue the Corrective Jerk as punishment. It is a line of communication that tells him he was incorrect.

When conducting teaching sessions never pet the dog as part of his praise. It must always be verbal otherwise it will virtually end the

Figure 3. Professional trainer, Linda Steigner of the National Institute of Dog Training, demonstrates the Corrective Jerk on *Spaghetti,* a very patient pupil.

1

lesson. The dog's attention span is narrow and any distraction will limit his learning capacity.

Do not feel embarrassed to praise the dog verbally when walking with him outdoors. It is very good for the dog and is not the least bit eccentric. Is it crazy to establish a full relationship with another living thing and make efforts to communicate? It is crazier not to. Many people, some of them scientists, claim they talk to their trees, shrubs, and plants and get better growing results by doing so. Establishing verbal rapport with a dog seems less peculiar. If one accepts the notion that love is a form of communication, then one need not express it in private little corners of a house. If a dog is corrected or if he performs properly he should be verbally praised no matter where he is at the time.

How hard to jerk the dog. In most cases we refer to a *firm jerk* throughout the command chapters of this book. By this we mean using both hands snapping the leash to the side with only that amount of force necessary to create a sensation around the animal's neck. It should not be so hard as to pull the dog off his legs or give him any pain whatsoever. It requires the same kind of deft handling as trying to pull the tablecloth out from under a fully set table so as not to disturb the dishes and silverware. Some animals are as fragile as fine china and should be handled as such.

When a *gentle jerk* is called for we mean the smallest amount of force possible that still creates some feeling around the animal's neck. The mildest sensation is all that is necessary. The accompanying "No" does most of the work. Jerk the leash delicately so that you can hear the collar snap like a zipper. The use of one hand is all that is really necessary for a gentle Corrective Jerk.

A *very firm* or *hard jerk* is rarely called for but when it is it must be delivered with greater than average force. This is sometimes used for a stubborn or aggressive dog of large stature. It is most useful before or during a fight between two dogs. Sometimes a *hard jerk* is the only thing that will move a dog that has dug in for full resistance to the training. In this case you must use both hands and great strength to establish who is in control of the situation. Even here, you must try not to hurt the dog.

Some dogs cry out, whine, or howl the first few times they meet the Corrective Jerk. Such noise has nothing to do with pain or abuse. It is an attempt to manipulate you into stopping the training. Some dogs are quite used to ruling their households and do not take it kindly when the owner tries to upset that *modus vivendi* with obedience training. Stand fast with a determined attitude and pay no attention to the dog's vocal protest. Train him in a secluded area.

Practice. It is not advisable to practice the Corrective Jerk on the dog. This is gratuitous from the dog's perspective and may make him jerk-shy. The Corrective Jerk must be viewed as a communicative tool that is used in conjunction with the commands taught in other chapters and not as a device unto itself. Use the arm of a member of the family as a substitute for the dog's neck when practicing. A banister or mop handle will also serve nicely. It would be unjust and even destructive to correct the dog for no reason at all. Never jerk a dog needlessly.

TEMPERAMENT TIPS

The nervous dog. When jerking a nervous dog the important factors are knowing when to correct, how hard to jerk, and when to stop and praise. If one excessively jerks a nervous dog he will resent it and offer resistance to all training. Never abuse the Corrective Jerk. The word "No" should always be used with great firmness when it accompanies a Corrective Jerk. Give the dog a chance to respond before repeating a correction. If the animal fights you after a correction by jumping up on you, stop the correction. You would be better advised to start off with gentle jerks and then slowly increase the power once the dog becomes accustomed to the technique. If the dog mouths your hand do not be frightened. Deliver a very firm correction and an extra-firm "No."

The nervous-shy dog. The Corrective Jerk should be used very sparingly on dogs of this temperament. Give slight tugs instead of firm jerks and speak softly and encouragingly. The dog will probably be frightened of the training in the beginning and firm corrections will alienate him. If you overjerk a nervous-shy dog you may never gain his trust or confidence again. A medium-to-small-size nervous-shy dog should never be worked with a metal choke collar. Use a nylon or leather choke collar. If the nervous-shy dog is the size of the toy breeds, do not use a choke collar at all.

The nervous-aggressive dog. Be very careful when using the Corrective Jerk. The dog may try to bite you when you turn your back. Do not jerk these dogs excessively. One firm jerk is much better than five or six mild jerks. Sometimes this type of dog will fight you by biting the leash or grabbing it with its paws. Use a hard Corrective Jerk and a firm "No." This is one temperament where the owner must be careful not to get bitten. If the dog is large, place the choke collar high up on his neck in order to achieve an effective Corrective Jerk. Be careful not to catch the dog's ears if they are long and flappy. The jerk should be quick and fast. The correction should take no longer than it takes to say, "Jerk-Release."

The shy dog. If the dog is very shy never use the Corrective Jerk at all. Use the word "No" gently, and, perhaps, tug the leash slightly. The biggest problem in training a shy dog is getting his confidence and making him feel playfully aggressive. An authoritative correction will make the dog regress in his training behavior. The objective here is to emphasize the teaching by spending more time with that part of the process so that fewer corrections will be necessary. More time in each lesson will be necessary this way but by the end of the course the dog will not only be better trained he will be more outgoing. Using the word "No" in a normal tone of voice is the only way to correct a shy dog.

The stubborn dog. This is the temperament that requires the Corrective Jerk the most. You must be very firm and demanding when jerking the stubborn dog. Often one jerk is not enough. You may have to give five or six in quick succession. Use the word "No" each time in a very loud tone of voice. One technique for the stubborn dog is to give him two Corrective Jerks in a row and then stop. See if he responds. If not, continue to correct the dog until he does respond properly. Very firm or hard jerks will get the point across to the dog much more quickly than ten halfhearted ones. In the case of a large stubborn dog, place the choke collar high up on his neck so that the jerk will be more effective. This is only recommended for exceptionally stubborn dogs of a large size. If the word "No" is used each and every time you correct the dog, and if your tone of voice is loud, you will eventually not have to jerk the dog at all. A verbal correction is all that will be necessary.

The sedate dog. The Corrective Jerk for this temperament will never have to be hard or firm. The word "No" should not be used authoritatively. A gentle jerk is all that should be used. Verbal corrections are much more valuable when training a sedate dog than Corrective Jerks. Because of the dog's lethargic manner he will have to be coaxed into training rather than forced. The tone of voice will do more to induce him to perform than anything else. Sometimes a sedate dog will not move at all if he is corrected harshly.

The aggressive dog. Here again you must determine if the dog is playfully aggressive or dangerously aggressive. When dealing with the latter you must be very hard on the animal if he attempts to bite you. By hard we mean jerking him as hard as possible. It will be much more effective if the choke collar is high on the dog's neck. If you jerk a dangerously aggressive dog harshly, he may respond in one of two ways. He'll either respond properly to the correction or he'll become wildly aggressive by biting the leash or clawing at it. He may even attempt to bite you. Each individual dog requires his owner's understanding of how far to go before he becomes uncontrollable. When jerking an aggressive dog (especially one over eighty pounds) watch for low throat growls and snarling lips. These are clear indications that the dog is going to bite. If the dog is unmanageable one should seek the services of a professional trainer.

On the other hand, the dog may be playfully aggressive. When you jerk him he will try to jump on you or mouth your hands but not in a dangerous way. It is more play than aggression. Be firm in your jerks and use an emphatic "No." In many ways this temperament is more responsive to training than others. Dogs of this temperament are lively and communicative and will respond to a firm Corrective Jerk. They are not dangerous at all.

10

WHAT MAKES SAMMY "*SIT*"?

"SIT" MEANS . . .

The dog will assume a sitting posture on command. The dog's body is upright with his front paws standing straight as his rear weight rests on his haunches. His hind legs are folded under his flanks and keep the front of his body erect. In the "Sit" position the dog looks straight ahead with a proud, upright demeanor.

FROM THE DOG'S POINT OF VIEW . . .

Dogs are very comfortable in a "Sit" position. They will often assume the position as a natural pose when they are observing something of interest or to facilitate scratching at some tucked-away corner of the body. However, getting them to go into a "Sit" position when you want them to is not of any great interest from their point of view. Unless the dog is watching you cook some very interesting food or is trying to get you out of bed in the morning he has not the slightest desire to sit.

Some dogs will practically yawn in your face as you keep repeating the order, "Sit! Sit! Sit!" They couldn't care less for your public image as a "dog person" or a fancier of sorts. If you do not know how to teach the animal to "Sit" on command and then execute the order, they behave as though it's your hard luck.

Some dog owners, only knowing a bit about dog obedience, will try to gain control over the animal with the use of the command "Sit." If the dog gets loose on the city street and you want to corner the animal you may hysterically yell, "Sit!" You are, obviously, on the right track. The problem is that the dog cannot go directly into a command from a state of excitement or distraction. He must first be corrected with a firm "No" and then he can be commanded, "Sit." Once the dog obeys he must then be praised. In this way the "Sit" can be utilized as a means of gaining control at a time when it might save the animal's life. Once the dog is taught the command properly he will always respond to it. He will not be able to refuse your command unless he is running at top speed or is involved in a dogfight. Even then, you may have just enough control to slow him down and get him away from the unpleasant situation.

The command "Sit" makes it clear to the dog what you expect of him in a given situation. Very often the doorbell will ring and the dog becomes either slaphappy over a potential visitor or turns into the family protector and growls and barks. In either case the dog must be controlled. "Sit" is the perfect command. It is a temporary position and readies the animal for any further commands.

HOW TO . . .

This is the first of the "command," chapters, therefore it is important to mention several items that will help facilitate the others. These items apply to every chapter that teaches a command. Unless the command is an action command, never say the dog's name before the order. Action commands involve forward motion ("Heel," "Come") and require that the dog's name be prefixed to the order. When the dog hears his name he should be alerted to forward motion.

It is important that the dog not be fed before a training session. If he is he will be sluggish and unable to learn. It is also a good idea to allow the animal to relieve himself before each training session. This is especially important if the session is going to be conducted outdoors. When the dog is taken outdoors his body immediately anticipates being able to empty itself. It is simply too distracting for him if he is not allowed this release.

As stressed in Chapter 2 there should be only one person who teaches each command to the dog. Once the dog has learned a given command it is desirable for the other members of the family also to learn how to execute the new command so that it is always done consistently. Always begin teaching something new in a quiet, secluded place. Whether going outdoors or indoors do not allow an audience to be present during the actual session. Last and perhaps most important, never hit the dog. Some animals learn more quickly than others and will try your patience when they slow down on a particular command. Do not become frustrated. There is no time limit set for the learning process. If you hit your dog, especially during the training period, you will seriously affect his temperament and render him untrainable.

Holding the leash. Teaching "Sit" requires two pieces of equipment: the choke collar and the six-foot training leash (preferably leather). Place the dog by your left side as you both face the same forward direction. The dog, it is assumed, is standing on all fours. The leash loosely dangles across your knees and up to your right hand. The thumb of the right hand is inserted into the very top of the loop while the rest of the hand clasps entirely around the loop. Next, gather all but two feet of the leash and include it in your grip. The gathered four feet of the leash hangs down your right leg in the form of one large loop. You are now in a position of maximum control over the dog.

Teaching "Sit." The next step after placing yourself and the dog in the proper position (and holding the leash correctly) is giving the vocal command. With a firm voice say, "Sit," and then gently push the dog's hindquarters down with your left hand. Keep pushing slowly until he has no choice but to be in a sitting position. (see Figure 4). In order to prevent the dog from being startled, do not push too hard or too fast. Otherwise, he will not stay in position. Once the dog has reached the sitting position give him lavish praise even though he did not get there on his own. It is the only way he knows what you expect of him. The praise is his reward for obeying your command. Remember, you are teaching something entirely new to the animal and going against his instincts. Therefore, you must be patient. When praising the dog do not pet him or make any body contact. It must all be done with a warm tone of voice just like that of a professional dog handler.

This command is quite easy to teach. You simply repeat the above fifteen or twenty times. By then the dog should be going into a "Sit" position without your pushing him into it. Your vocal command "Sit" will suffice. Do not correct the dog for any reason during this teaching period. Introducing a negative note while teaching something new will only make the dog have a negative association with the new command. This is important.

Correcting the dog is allowed once he has learned the command. After being taught "Sit" or any other command the dog will, from time to time, refuse to obey your order. It is then appropriate to administer a Corrective Jerk accompanied by a firm "No." Give him immediate praise after the dog responds to the correction.

The first teaching session requires that you repeat the command twenty times. After that, allow the dog a short rest and then repeat the command another twenty times. During the rest period do not allow the animal to decide that the lesson is over for the day. That is accomplished by avoiding any play or extensive walks. By the second half of the training session the dog should have learned "Sit" by vocal command only. If not, one more entire session will be necessary but not without one hour rest, at the very least.

A training formula. Once a dog has gone through the teaching process of any command and you feel that he has actually learned what you taught, he may no longer ignore your order. It is time to employ the Corrective Jerk whenever he refuses to obey your command. There is a formula that is very helpful in remembering the order of training techniques. It is quite simply Command, Correction, and Praise. This only applies, of course, when the dog does not obey on the first command. The correction is a reminder that he must obey the command he just heard. Once the animal responds, praise him. It is important to the training that the dog be praised

Figure 4. The correct way to teach "Sit" is demonstrated by author Matthew Margolis. Cooperating is Chow-Husky mix, *Herschel*. Verbal command, "Sit," is given as dog is lowered into position by applying pressure on rear haunches. Notice firm, taut leash control.

2

3

immediately after a proper response to a command or correction. This is an integral part of the teaching process.

TEMPERAMENT TIPS

The nervous dog. Teaching "Sit" to a nervous dog will at first result in excitement and distraction. Therefore, conduct the lesson in the privacy of your home or fenced-off backyard. When placing your hand on the animal's back to push him into a sitting position make sure that the leash (held in the right hand) is very taut so the dog will not be able to turn around or move. Sometimes a dog may try to nip or bite your hand. For this reason beware of the intensity of pressure on his back with your hand. Try to push down as quickly as possible so he won't have time to react negatively. When he responds, praise the dog with both voice and hands. Another teaching technique for the nervous dog is to stroke his back with your hand before attempting to push him down. Allow the dog to become accustomed to the feel of your hand before pushing him. Because of his nervousness it will be a strange and scary situation for the dog. Be patient and understanding. One last technique for keeping the nervous dog in position so he won't move is to lean your body against his. That will help him to remain stationary.

The shy dog. Make sure the dog is taught in a private place. Always use a soothing tone of voice and give the command "Sit" very softly and lovingly. If the dog becomes frightened when you stand over him, try kneeling. From your knees push the dog's rump down gently until he reaches a sitting position. If he tries to run away do not jerk him or hold him back. Simply return him to the training as gently as you can. Speak very soothingly to him and then try again. You will give the dog confidence and abate his fears if you are very verbal and physical in your reassurance. Be very patient and take as much time as is necessary. Because he is shy your presence standing over him or kneeling down and pushing his rump may scare him.

The stubborn dog. Time and patience are very important with this temperament. The dog may bring you to the emotional state where you will want to hit him. Resist these emotions. Some stubborn dogs will fight you and not stand in the "Heel" position prior to the lesson. One of the best remedies for this is exercise. Run off his excessive energy and tire him out somewhat. Then place him in position and utilize firm leash control as you push him into the "Sit" position. If he tries to move around, use your body to keep him stationary and tighten up on the leash. One of his tricks may be to jump up on you as you push him down to "Sit". In this case you have no alternative but to use the Corrective Jerk accompanied by a firm "No." He may start whining or crying just to see if he can get away with it. Steel yourself and do not give in to emotional blackmail. The dog is simply testing you. If you are patient and persistent you will win both the battle and the war.

The sedate dog. The biggest problem will be the dog's desire to lie down instead of going into a "Sit" position. Use a great deal of verbal praise to keep his attention and do not feed him before the lesson. Do not jerk the dog or pull him if he lies down. Pick him up with your hands gently and place him in a standing position and begin again. The sedate dog may appear aloof and distant when you attempt to conduct a training session. He simply is not being receptive to the idea of training as something that will reward him. Give him a great deal of praise and break up the training sessions with enthusiastic play.

The aggressive dog. In teaching "Sit" to an aggressive dog you must determine if his aggressiveness is more playful than dangerous. When teaching "Sit" to a playfully aggressive dog you can expect him to jump around, pull at the leash, and, in short, not take the session very seriously. Do not mistake this behavior as indicating a bad dog. He is simply very exuberant. The way to control him is to maintain firm leash control. If the animal persists in jumping, administer a Corrective Jerk and a firm "No." Immediately after the correction place him in the standing position, say, "Sit!" and push down on his rump in a very firm manner.

If the dog is aggressively dangerous and he attempts to bite you, give him very strong Corrective Jerks and very loud "No's." If he will not let you touch his rump, stand in front of him and pull upward on the leash, forcing his head and neck back so as to make him sit. Lavish him with praise immediately afterward. If he still continues to resist with aggressively dangerous behavior, seek professional help. It is not worth a possible injury.

The responsive dog. If your dog has a responsive temperament, follow the lesson plan as outlined in the beginning of the chapter.

11

PUT YOUR FAITH IN THE
HEELER   *("Heel" and "Heel-Sit")*

"HEEL" MEANS . . .

The dog must walk when given the command and carefully pace himself so that he never pulls ahead or lags behind. He is on the left side of his master with his head approximately next to the left knee.

FROM THE DOG'S POINT OF VIEW . . .

Life is nothing but ankles and shoes, rolling auto tires, very small children, curbstones, fire hydrants, discarded chewing-gum wrappers, and sidewalk cracks from the dog's-eye view. What a dog sees when taken outdoors is not even the half of his sensual experience. His incredible sense of smell has virtually thousands of different scents to experience and his keen hearing gets its most vigorous workout outdoors. It is little wonder that dogs seem to go wild with joy when they see their leashes and collars. Being taken out for a walk is probably the most important part of the day, next to being fed, and no dog can resist the oncoming pleasures. In the case of a puppy it is even more heightened because everything is so new. Going outside represents a heady sense of adventure, curiosity, play, and digestive release (no small matter). The problem is that in their enthusiasm all the dear dogs in the world make their owners miserable with the pulling and tugging and jumping. A medium-to-large-size animal can dislocate a woman's shoulder if she is taken by surprise when the dog lunges at the brute across the street.

What does an untrained dog know about walking gently by his owner's side and stopping when the owner stops? The dog has no idea that he can enjoy his walk equally as well if he calmly keeps pace with his master. But this is something that can and must be taught because it affects the safety of the dog and the serenity of the owner. To walk: perchance to "Heel": ay, there's the ticket: For in that walk what pleasures may come . . . (with apologies to Hamlet).

About walking. Obviously, walking is one of the most natural acts for all dogs. But walking in "Heel" is something the dog must be taught. The dog will eventually acquire a taste for going out in this manner. However, in the beginning, especially during the teaching process, he is not going to like it at all. Every natural instinct and impulse will be thwarted. Therefore, if the sessions are held outdoors take him to a quiet, secluded place with as few distractions as possible. Allow the dog to relieve himself before starting and then expect him to be confused at the teaching process. He will want to go exploring while you force him to pay keen attention to you as you take him through the heeling paces.

It is important that the dog maintain his happy mood when taken outside for a lesson in heeling. He must not come to dread his training sessions. This will depend on how well you communicate a good feeling to him. What is required is a special language between you and the animal. It all has to do with vocal intonation. A harsh sound will produce a remorseful reaction from the dog. A cool, firm sound produces an attentive, alert reaction. But high-pitched praise similar to baby talk excites the animal and makes him joyful. The words themselves are almost of no consequence at all. It is the tone of voice that matters. The same thing applies when talking to a human baby. The baby has no comprehension of language as it pertains to words and their meaning. It is all vocal but not necessarily verbal. A dog, just like a baby, responds to communicated emotion.

HOW TO . . .

Getting ready for the "Heel." It is no longer necessary to begin movements from a standing position now that "Sit" has been taught. The correct starting position is very important and should always be used when commanding the dog to "Heel." First, place the dog in the "Sit" position and be certain he is on your left side. This is the traditional side for a dog to "Heel". It must always be used consistently. The left side was originally determined by men who took their dogs on hunting trips and wanted them away from the rifle.

The leash. In no command is the proper position of the leash more important than in "Heel." With two feet of leash draped across the front of your knees, hold it firmly in the right hand, which must always be comfortably situated next to your right thigh. Holding the least for "Heel" is exactly as it is depicted in Chapter 9, "The Corrective Jerk." During the teaching of this command it will be necessary to use both hands to hold the leash so that firm jerks can be implemented (see Chapter 9, "Holding the Leash Properly").

Starting out with the left foot. Because "Heel" is an action command, you must use the dog's name before saying the command word itself. Using the dog's name alerts him to forward motion and allows him the slight pause necessary to respond properly. Saying the dog's name also gets his attention so he will focus on you, ready to move forward. The full command should be, "Horatio, [pause] heel." Then walk forward, starting out with the *left* foot. This is important because the dog sees your left foot first. When it moves so will he. You will then be starting out together and that is the beginning of the correct "Heel" (see Figure 5).

Running ahead. It is safe to assume that the dog, in his untrained state, will run ahead because that is what he has always done. Right from the beginning your first objective is to break him of this behavior. Allow him to run ahead, using up the full length of the six-foot leash. Make a fast right turn when he gets to the end of it. The dog will be pulled hard and it will surprise him. At the instant of maximum stress repeat the vocal command, "Horatio, heel." Without a moment's pause quickly walk in the opposite direction,

1

2

Figure 5. To get a dog to "Heel" properly you must start walking with your left foot. Maintain firm leash control and keep the dog's attention on you.

3

4

being sure that the leash is on your left side. The dog will have no choice but to turn and walk in your direction as he stumbles along to catch up. When he does, give him lavish praise. This will require a firm assertion of your will over the dog's.

Do not stop or slow down. The dog will overcome his confusion and eventually catch up with you. Praise him and readjust the leash to the length with which you started. Most certainly the dog will run ahead again. Repeat the technique with absolutely no regard for his whines or even screams. Some dogs are criers and will try to make you stop what you are doing. Do not respond to it because it is a ploy to control you rather than the other way around. You will not be hurting him. For this reason it is desirable to train the animal in a secluded area, free from the criticism of those who will mistakenly think you are abusing him. Be assured that the dog is not being hurt when you change your direction and walk away. We cannot emphasize enough the importance of the praise when the dog catches up. The turning procedure is hard on his psyche and he is not sure if you are angry with him. It is very important that he *does not* think you are angry. The praise helps to guide him. He will soon associate walking by your side with your approval.

Keeping up with you. Some dogs tend to lag behind their masters and make their walks a series of stops and starts. It's a form of sniffing behind your back. Either the dog has always done it or he has developed the habit after being taught not to run ahead. This new behavior will start after two or three heeling lessons when the dog has stopped darting forward. This is one problem that should be solved with verbal communication. Don't be ashamed to talk to your dog. Dog talk works and is the best answer to this problem. Playfully encourage the animal to walk with you, to catch up, to keep pace. If the sound of your voice is enthusiastic and friendly the dog will bound to you and then keep his attention upward on your face. This is exactly what to work for. When the dog is in "Heel" he should be focused on you, ready for your next move or command.

"Heeling" correctly. The exact position for "Heel" is by your left side; the dog's head is approximately next to your left knee. After several lessons it becomes important to maintain exactitude. In the

early lessons the dog will have done all right if he only stayed two or three feet ahead. It is now time that he be corrected whenever he strays from the correct place.

This teaching process begins with the dog in "Sit." He is by your left side. Give the command, "Milton, heel." Begin walking with your left foot. Maintain firm leash control with both hands so that you can execute a Corrective Jerk firmly. Do not allow more than two feet of leash to drape across your knees. Once you start to move it is important that the dog be made to keep pace and remain in the correct relationship with your left knee.

Whenever the dog fails to maintain the exact, correct position, do the following: Jerk the dog firmly, say, "Alice, heel!," execute a right turn, and walk in the opposite direction. Give the dog immediate praise. The praise keeps the dog informed that you are not angry and that he is now doing the correct thing. Do this again and again and again throughout each lesson until the animal is heeling in the true sense of the command. In makeing these repeated right turns the use of body language can be an excellent added dimension to the teaching process. Moving with a light touch (like a gymnast) will keep the dog alert and in a learning frame of mind. Walk briskly, with precision, like a man or woman knowing where you are going. Spring on the balls of the feet. Turn sharply and authoritatively. All this helps to establish the dog-master relationship that is so necessary in obedience training. The livelier you are, the more responsive you make the dog.

HEELING PROBLEMS

Wrapping himself around your legs. This ridiculous sight is often seen when a dog is smothered with affection throughout every day and expects more even though he is being walked. Sometimes the animal is insecure or overly sensitive and seeks the protection of his master and consequently wraps himself around the owner's legs, inadvertently.

This problem will have to be solved with care and gentleness.

Begin walking in "Heel" and hold the animal in the proper position with your left hand. Do not correct him and avoid harsh or negative sounds. On the contrary, give the dog praise and encouragement as you walk and hold him in the proper position. In the beginning walk slowly and methodically. Make gentle turns as you maintain a firm grip on the leash with the right hand. Hold the dog in place with the left hand. It is most important that the animal learn the proper "Heel" position in the beginning. Therefore, do not make corrections during this time-consuming teaching process. Gentleness and affectionate speech will help end this problem.

Jumping. An energetic and friendly dog will climb all over someone he encounters while out for his walk. This is especially true if he spots a favorite person or a stranger who needs some affection himself. It is amazing how many "dog lovers" one meets (total strangers) who will stop and make a fuss over a dog they have never met. They are willing to offer gratuitous affection (and interrupt a training session) but rarely will assume the responsibility for giving an animal a home. Bad advice and ill-timed horsing around is usually thrown in for good measure. Don't fall for it. Let the person get his own dog. Keep moving and maintain the obedience lesson or the walk.

It should be established that the dog is never allowed to jump on anyone. Once that is firmly set in your mind you must stick to it, especially during the teaching of "Heel." When the dog tosses the front part of his body on someone, anyone, execute a Corrective Jerk and sharply say, "No!" This must be enforced at all times whether indoors or outdoors.

Walking at an angle. During the teaching of "Heel" some dogs will fail to negotiate a straight line and will turn inward toward your legs. This impossible situation results in both dog and owner stepping on one another. There is no known reason for this behavior unless it is physiological. The average, healthy dog who does this has simply not learned to walk the straight and narrow path. Here again, the solution lies in the Corrective Jerk.

When the animal begins walking at an angle, execute a Corrective Jerk, say "No" in a firm voice, and make a right turn. Force the dog to turn with you. Once the dog is walking straight again, give him praise for doing the right thing. Immediately follow the praise with the verbal command, "Helen, heel!" Praise her again. Repeat this procedure every time the dog walks a crooked line.

Left turn in "Heel." If the dog is walking slightly ahead of you, a good way of correcting him is to make a left turn. This is accomplished by giving the command, "Morris, heel!" On the word "Heel" jerk the leash to the right, wait a split second, and execute a left turn. If the correction is properly done, the dog will look up at you and enable you to walk in front of him and around to the left (see Figure 6). Do not pull or jerk on the leash when you begin the turn or you may trip over it and/or the dog. This also applies to a right turn in "Heel" (see Figure 7). The most important aspect is that you not jerk the leash as you make the actual turn. First jerk the leash, pause a second, then execute the turn.

TEMPERAMENT TIPS

The nervous dog. "Heel" is the most difficult command for dogs of this temperament. It should be taught in a quiet area with *no* distractions. Once the dog has learned the basics he may then be given lessons in a public place. The nervous dog will not be very atttentive; therefore it is important to execute very firm leash corrections. The corrections should be given fast and frequently so as to keep his attention and teach him in the shortest period of time possible. Always let the dog pull on the leash. Do not try to pull the dog back. Use the entire length of the leash when making corrections. You will then get a better correction and the animal will respond quicker. Use a great deal of praise after each technique of teaching and certainly after each and every correction. If the nervous dog is a puppy do not be too hard on him. The corrections must be gentle. Spend extra time in the teaching process. This command will be the hardest for the nervous dog. It requires patience for the teacher.

An added dimension for teaching this command to the nervous dog is the use of agile body movement. Changing the pace of the

5

Figure 6. Executing a left turn while in "Heel" can be awkward. Give the verbal command,

6

"Herschel, heel!" Jerk the leash to the right, wait a split second, then turn left.

Figure 7. How to execute a right turn while walking in "Heel."

walk in "Heel" from brisk to slow and back to brisk keeps the animal alert. Make left turns then right turns, stop and start, run with the dog and then stop suddenly. The more varied body movements you perform, the more attentive the dog will be.

The nervous-shy dog. Dogs of this temperament will not only be reticent about walking, they may also put up the fight of their lives to stay put. They will be terrorized by the outdoors and any movement into it. Do not be frightened if the dog starts screaming or whining. You are not hurting him. Simply be sure to conduct the lessons in a quiet, secluded location free from the criticism of misguided hysterics who do not understand dog behavior or obedience training. No one but the teacher may be present.

The nervous-shy dog will resist movement by jumping or clawing at the leash. Do not be too hard on the dog. Keep walking in a forward direction and try to keep the animal on your left side. Give him lavish praise and encouragement. If necessary, drop to your knees and call the dog to you with enthusiasm and playfulness. Get him to come to you. Do this several times, until he comes every time you bend down. Then begin backing away as he comes to you. Eventually, you may rise to your feet, make a turn, and walk away together.

Do not make the mistake of dragging the dog along a hard, paved surface. This may tear the skin of his pads and cause him pain and bleeding. Once this happens it will be next to impossible to get the dog to "Heel" without a neurotic reaction. If you see a struggle about to ensue be sure the dog is taught on a grassy surface to avoid any medical/emotional problems.

Another possibility is that the dog may defecate during this process. Do not be alarmed. It is a physical expression of fear. Terminate the lesson and try again the next day. The key to teaching "Heel" to a nervous-shy dog is patience and understanding. Imagine yourself at the dog's end of the leash so that you are better able to understand the problem from his point of view. Spend all the time necessary for teaching your nervous-shy dog. One last suggestion for puppies of this temperament: Allow them to walk around the house for several hours a day with the leash connected to the collar. (Never without the owner watching, of course). This will allow them to get used to it and not fear it when going outside for the lesson.

The nervous-aggressive dog. He will probably try jumping on you or mouth your hands when you begin walking in "Heel." Administer Corrective Jerks for this behavior and continue walking. After the corrections the dog may start talking back and growling. Instead of repeating the jerks it is advisable to change directions rapidly and in quick succession when walking. This will keep the animal too busy to continue his objections to the lesson. Praise the dog but use a mellow tone of voice depending on his degree of aggressiveness. Exuberant praise is often taken as a signal to a very aggressive dog to continue his bad behavior.

If the animal is aggressive toward other dogs when being taught "Heel," keep the choke collar high on his neck. Deliver three or four firm Corrective Jerks accompanied by a firm "No." The high placement of the collar makes the jerks much more effective.

A young puppy may snap when being taught "Heel." Give him one Corrective Jerk and wait a few seconds before moving. He may be apologetic and approach you, trying to curry your favor. In that case give him lavish praise. If he continues his aggressive behavior give him another Corrective Jerk (not too hard) and wait for his reaction. He should respond positively.

The shy dog. This behavior is manifested by the animal's refusal to walk when first taken outside. It is true of many puppies. They are afraid of the outdoors and seek the protection of your legs or the nearest wall. Do not be authoritative or harsh. Attempt to rid the dog of his fear by praising him and encouraging him to walk in "Heel." If this fails you must place yourself in front of him and drop to your knees. Make a game out of calling the animal to you. Call him by name and lavish him with praise every step of the way. Get him to come to you. Do this several times, until he comes every time you bend down. The next step is to start backing away as the dog comes to you. Get him moving forward for longer distances until such time as you can rise to your feet without making the dog hesitate. Once this happens, make a turn with the dog on your left side and walk away in the "Heel" position. You may now start teaching as outlined in the beginning of this chapter.

Do not teach this command on a hard surface. If the dog resists walking he may hurt his pads and forever fear walking in "Heel." Conduct these lessons on a soft, grassy surface. It may even be advisable to start teaching "Heel" indoors just to help the dog learn the basics before being forced to deal with his fear. Be patient with a shy dog. Never use the word "No" or hard jerks when teaching a dog of this temperament or you will only add to his shyness. Allow the dog to wander or pull ahead in the beginning. This will aid in overcoming his shy behavior.

The stubborn dog. When this kind of dog runs to the end of his leash during the first "Heel" lesson he may do one or all of the following: He may start to fight you by pulling away, clawing at the leash with his paws, or talking back with growls and barks. This is an "I'll do what I want, when I want" attitude. When you step off on your left foot, the dog may not respond or make any attempt to heel. The harder you correct him the more stubborn he may become. The answer here is to place the choke collar high up on the animal's neck, jerk him, and say, "King, heel!" He may still try to fight you but he will feel the pressure on his neck and respond more quickly. If he starts to rear up and fight, relax the leash. When he stops, give the "Heel" command, jerk him, and begin walking. This technique is not suggested for young puppies and small dogs. Only employ it if the animal is one year old or older. Be careful with dogs who have tender necks such as Afghan mixes, Dalmatian mixes, Terrier mixes, Dachsund mixes, Boxer mixes and Pug mixes. Obviously, a dog with a small, frail body cannot be dealt with in this manner. Patience and persistence are your only tools in that situation.

Always use active and varied body movements with a stubborn dog so that he stays attentive. Do not be fooled by your dog's stubbornness. It is not a lack of intelligence. Some of the brightest dogs are among the most stubborn. If the lesson is very hard on the dog, the teacher should stop and continue ten minutes later. Teach this command in privacy.

The sedate dog. The most common problem for dogs of this temperament is lagging behind. Give the dog a great deal of verbal praise and use a wide variety of body movements such as quick changes of pace, starts and stops, turns, etc. When teaching this type of dog the "Heel," try running with the dog. This may generate enthusiasm in the dog and create the feeling of fun. Do not jerk him very hard and talk to him a great deal. In this case, distraction may be the best medicine. Use his name very often and employ varied body movements to keep his attention on you. The more excitement you can create, the more lively the dog will be.

The aggressive dog. When teaching "Heel," be on guard when you jerk a dog of this temperament. He may try to jump on you or bite your hand. In starting the "Heel," let the dog run ahead, then jerk him but do not turn around. Do not turn your back on him. Let him go to the end of the leash as you stand facing him, then jerk him. He may try to bite the leash or hold it down with his paws. Leave some slack in the leash and praise him if it calms him down. Be very verbal in your praise and avoid petting him. Before starting be sure that the choke collar is placed high on the dog's neck. In this way if he begins to snarl, growl, or turns to bite, you are in a position to execute a very firm Corrective Jerk, swing him around, or suspend him off the ground in order to gain control. Although this sounds very harsh, you cannot afford to make too many mistakes with an aggressive dog that may weigh as much as 50 to 125 pounds. It is important to note that the average dog has approximately 500 to 1,000 pounds of pressure in his jaws when he decides to bite. By suspending the animal we mean holding the leash with both hands so that the dog's front paws are off the ground. This should last three seconds (if necessary at all). Release the dog and then go into the "Heel" command. It is important to establish firm control over the dog and command his respect without hurting him. An aggressive dog can be like a loaded gun ready to go off at any time. You must always have a countermeasure ready for his difficult behavior. It is a battle of wits and will. Always maintain control and authority and never back down. If the dog frightens you, do not let him know it. Train him in a private area with no distractions. One should consider having this type of dog trained by a professional.

"HEEL-SIT" MEANS . . .

When walking in "Heel" the dog will respond to a stop by going into the "Sit" position. The dog stops every time the master does and sits without being commanded to do so.

HOW TO . . .

This is accomplished by alerting the dog that a stop is coming up very soon. The signal for stopping is quite simple. You merely reduce your speed of walking. If the dog is focused on you, as he should be, he will be sensitive to any change of pace. As you slow down, so will the dog.

During the teaching process give the dog the command "Sit" every time you stop. As you verbally give the command raise the leash tautly above his head twelve inches. Assuming he has already learned the command "Sit," this is all that is necessary. Repeat this procedure many times until he sits without the verbal command. Never use the dog's name when giving this command. "Sit" is not an action command and you do not want any forward motion when giving it. Every time the dog sits on command give him his well-deserved praise.

Failure to obey. If the dog does not "Heel-Sit" after he has been taught to do so, you may execute a Corrective Jerk and a firm "No!" It is not fair to correct a dog before he has been taught what to do. But after one or two lessons it can be assumed that he knows what to do and is simply testing your authority or is disinterested or is forgetful. In either case the Corrective Jerk and the sharp "No" remind him what to do. Praise the dog immediately after he has obeyed the command, even though he had to be corrected.

Occasionally a dog will not even respond to the Corrective Jerk when commanded to "Sit" from the "Heel" position. Repeat the Corrective Jerk (firmly) and give him the command "Sit." Pull the leash twelve inches above the dog's head and push his haunches down into a sitting position with your left hand. This technique must be used only as a last resort. It is never a good idea to give a command following a Corrective Jerk. It can create a bad association for the dog. He must always anticipate praise with every command given rather than correction.

It should not take too many corrections and repetitions for the dog to execute the "Heel-Sit" properly and without benefit of verbal commands. It is impressive and gratifying to walk down a street with your dog in perfect "Heel" and have him stop and sit as you wait for the traffic light to turn green or if you decide to stop and talk to someone. "Heel-Sit" is the whipped cream on the cake.

End every lesson on a high note of praise so that the dog will anticipate his next with pleasure. The way to do this is to finish each session when the animal obeys the new command (or any part of it) correctly for the first time. Convey to him your exuberant pleasure and allow him to squirt on the most convenient vertical object.

12

"SIT-STAY"

"SIT-STAY" MEANS . . .

As in "Sit," the dog assumes a sitting posture on command. His body is upright with his front legs straight as his rear weight rests on his haunches. The dog's hind legs are folded under his flanks and keep the front of his body erect. He looks straight ahead and moves very little. After being given the proper verbal command and hand signal he must hold that position until he is released by his master (see Figure 8).

FROM THE DOG'S POINT OF VIEW . . .

Just because you have commanded a dog to "Sit" is no reason why he can't move on to more interesting matters such as what's cookin' on the stovetop, a ringing doorbell, or the cat's examination of his food bowl. As long as the dog has met his initial obligation to sit for you he is as free as the wind to go about his more important business. He is, unless he's been taught the command "Stay." When placed in "Sit" and then commanded "Stay," the dog should not move an inch from the spot until his master says, "Okay."

The advantages to his command are obviously great and there isn't a dog owner in the world who wouldn't appreciate them. From the dog's point of view, however, the feeling is different. No dog is

Figure 8. Professional trainers demonstrate "Sit-Stay."

naturally inclined to remain in a "Sit" position when there is something else he would rather do. Only the obedience-trained animal experiences any pleasure from it at all. Once the dog has been trained, his reward system has been altered so that he willingly works very hard to receive his master's praise. Although there is no way to measure it, the trained animal much perfers human approval to anything else, save food, elimination, and sex.

A dog trained to "Stay" will not run out of the house the minute the door is opened once he has been given the correct and appropriate command. Although it's almost impossible to keep puppies from following you around, a young or mature dog can be given the "Stay" command and be expected to stay out from underfoot. Of course, if there is a large social gathering in the house a dog may have a nervous collapse trying to obey the command "Stay" while trying to satisfy his curiosity and his sense of fair play. Its only fair to invite the dog to join the festivities or take him to a very remote area. The same applies when you're cooking. Do not leave tantalizing food within the animal's reach and then place him in "Stay." It would take a truly exceptional dog to maintain his discipline and not go for a cooked roast or steak. It is a fact, however, that many a trained dog has resisted that temptation. Nevertheless, it is not a good idea to test the dog in this manner.

Dogs do not enjoy remaining in a "Sit-Stay" position for long periods of time. It is not as comfortable as lying down or moving around. Do not abuse this command by expecting the dog to remain in "Sit-Stay" for hours. A well-trained animal should not be expected to remain in position for more than fifteen or thirty minutes. Even at that, it takes a very well trained dog to hold still for that amount of time.

Another qualification and limitation for this command is its use outdoors and off-leash. There is nothing a dog loves better than to be outdoors, free to roam and explore. And it seems to be every dog owner's fantasy to have his pet run around without a leash and then by magic have the dog freeze in one position when given the command. In our opinion it is too risky to attempt it with the average dog whether in the city or in the country. There is now almost as high a percentage of cars in the rural areas per capita as there is in the city. The fatality rate for dogs killed by automobiles in the city and the country is staggering. Every other dog owner has a story to tell that is painfully sad and aggravating to hear because in every case a leash would have kept the dog alive. *The most responsive dogs in the world with the best training available cannot be relied upon to hold a position outdoors each and every time without some physical restraint.* A dog may break once out of a thousand times but that may be just once too many times. It is simply not worth the chance to place a dog in "Sit-Stay" outdoors while off the leash. A rabbit or squirrel on the other side of the road or a dog in heat across the street are all it takes to set a dog in flight without any regard to traffic or other hazards. It is erroneous and archaic to say that a dog must be free to roam around or he isn't in a natural state. It is more natural for him to be alive enjoying life with his family.

"Sit-Stay" must be taught indoors and with the use of the six-foot training leash. One does not teach the command outdoors without the use of the twenty-foot clothesline and not until the dog has mastered the command on the six-foot line.

HOW TO . . .

Teaching "Sit-Stay" requires the use of three techniques. The first is a verbal command. The second is a hand signal. The third is a turning movement on the ball of the left foot.

Verbal command. With the dog on your left side both you and the animal are facing in the same direction. Give him the command, "Sit!" Praise him after he goes into the proper position. Next, give him the command, "Stay!" The hand signal accompanies the verbal command.

Hand signal. Hold the leash with your right hand and allow enough to drape across your knees so there is a little slack plus the width of your body. The signal is given with the left hand. Flatten your left hand and keep all fingers straight and close together as if you were going to use it for swimming. As you give the command,

"Stay," place your left hand in front of the dog's eyes leaving about four inches of space so that you never touch them. The hand signal is accomplished quickly and merely blocks the dog's vision for a second. Return your left hand to your side one or two seconds after blocking the dog's vision. Eventually, the dog will remain in the "Stay" with the use of the hand signal exclusively.

Turning on the left foot. The objective is to make a pivotal turn so that you will face the dog without stirring him as you effect the turn. To accomplish this you use the left foot as a pivot and do not move it from its original position. Step off with your right foot and turn to face the animal. Allow your left foot to revolve in place as your right foot moves forward one step so that you are almost facing the dog. After you have placed the right foot on the ground, facing the dog, move the left foot next to it so that you have accomplished the complete turn and are now facing the dog (see Figure 9). If you do this any other than the prescribed way, the dog will assume you are about to say "Heel" and start moving.

How to teach "Stay." While effecting the pivotal turn maintain the leash eighteen inches straight above the dog's head. The leash should be taut so that the animal cannot move as you turn to face him. It is not productive to keep the leash too tight because that might frighten the dog and make him want to run away. It is this firm leash control that forces the dog to associate remaining in position with the verbal command, "Stay."

Give the dog very little time to think about all this. From the beginning of the verbal command "Stay" to the hand signal and the pivotal turn only a few seconds should have gone by. This should be repeated fifteen times. Always praise the dog after successfully completing each and every turn despite the fact that he had to be held in place with the leash. Part of the teaching process is standing in front of the dog for a full twenty seconds after effecting each turn. The idea of remaining in "Stay" will be absorbed by the dog and a conditioned reflex to the command will begin to develop. The pivotal turn is merely a teaching tool and will not be used after the dog has learned the command completely.

Back away. It is now time to back away as the dog remains in

"Stay." Give the verbal command, "Stay," accompany it with the hand signal, make a turn so that you are facing the dog. Maintain the eighteen inches of leash tautly above the dog's head with the right hand. Once you are standing in front of the dog place the leash in your left hand and grasp the leash as in the Corrective Jerk. The right hand then grasps only the main line of the leash, directly under the left hand, and holds it loosely. As you back away, the leash should be able to slide freely through the right hand allowing it to extend. This prevents any slack from developing as you back away. This is important so that you will be able to correct the dog if he tries to move out of position as you back away.

You now should commence backing away from the dog. The leash slides through your right hand as it is held firmly by the left and gets longer as you move backward. The dog may begin to walk toward you as you move away. If he does, give him the verbal command, "Stay," and move in toward him. Pull the leash through your right hand as you move forward and hold it once again eighteen inches above his head. The leash must always be taut so as to force the dog to remain in the "Sit" position. Always pull the leash slightly to the side as you move in so you avoid hitting the dog with the metal clip. Stepping toward the dog will stop him from moving. Once the dog has stopped moving he must be praised. Pause for several seconds and then begin backing away again. Keep moving until the dog tries to move. You may get back a little farther this time. Repeat the procedure. Step in toward the dog as you pull the leash through your right hand, keeping it taut and above the dog's head. Praise him for stopping and wait several seconds before moving away. Continue this technique until you can back away a full six feet (the length of the leash) while the dog sits in "Stay." Once the dog will "Stay" for the entire length of the six-foot leash, repeat the process fifteen times.

Walking to the side of the dog. The objective here is to teach the dog to remain in "Stay" as you walk to either side of him without his moving out of position. It would be a violation of the command if the dog turned his entire body around to watch you as you walked to his right or left side after placing him in "Stay." Most dogs will turn

Figure 9. Pupil, *Butch,* is taught "Sit-Stay."

Trainer gives hand signal for "Stay"

3

uses his left foot as a pivot

so that he can turn to face the
dog without making him move .

4

their heads to watch and that is permissible if not perfect behavior. The animal must never be allowed to move his entire body around once he has been put in "Stay"; otherwise, the discipline of this command will deteriorate and it will be rendered unreliable.

Place the dog in "Sit." Give him the command, "Stay." Accompany the "Stay" with the hand signal and execute the pivotal turn as you hold the leash eighteen inches tautly above the dog's head. Step once or twice to the right as you hold the dog in place. Return to the original position directly in front of the dog. Now do the same to the left. Return to position. Repeat this ten times. Having accomplished this, repeat the entire lesson up to this point five or ten times, until you are satisfied that the dog has absorbed everything.

Walking around the dog. With the dog on your left side, place him in "Sit." Give him the verbal command, "Stay," and the hand signal. Effect the pivotal turn and stand in front of the animal as you maintain eighteen inches of leash tautly above his head. Hold the leash with your left hand as your right grasps the leash directly underneath it. Hold the dog in place as you walk around him, making a complete circle. If the dog moves, tighten up on the leash and say, "Stay!" Reassure the dog with a cool tone of voice offering praise and encouragement. Take large steps. Work the leash with finesse as you extend it when around the dog's back and take it back in as you come around to his front. Never allow any slack in the leash and maneuver it about so that you maintain absolute control over the animal. Tighten the leash every time the dog tries to move and release it slightly when he settles down. Praise him every time he settles down. Leash control is very important. It helps develop in the dog a total respect for the owner's authority. The idea of the leash remains in the dog's mind for his entire life as an abstraction. The dog always thinks of himself as connected to the leash even when it is not on him.

"Stay" is a difficult command for your dog. It will not be easy for him or you. It is therefore suggested that you not attempt to teach the entire command in one session. Take all the time that is necessary for the dog to absorb the material completely and without fail. If you go too fast the dog may please you by performing once but may fail to remember what he was taught by the next day. It is well worth the effort to be patient and teach each phase of this command slowly and carefully.

OUTDOORS AND OFF-LEASH

"Stay" off-leash while outdoors is very difficult for the dog to learn and it takes a long time to teach it. Although we do not recommend this command for outdoor use some dog owners feel that their living conditions are safe enough to take advantage of it. A fenced-off area or remote locale are the only types of places one should attempt to teach "Stay" off-leash.

Using a clothesline in place of a leash. Teaching this command outdoors will require the use of a twenty-five-foot line. It cannot be emphasized enough, however, that the dog be fully responsive to "Stay" with the six-foot leash as outlined above. It will be a great waste of time to go any further if the dog is not absolutely perfect on the preliminary work. It is impossible to cut corners when teaching "Stay" off-leash.

Teaching the same way. There is only one difference between teaching "Stay" on- or off-leash. The techniques are the same except that you extend the length of the leash two feet at a time every time the dog holds his position perfectly for the front, back, side, and circular movements.

It will be necessary to take up some of the leash every time you walk behind the dog's back in the circular movement. Slide it through the right hand as you take it up. This is done so that you will be able to correct the dog quickly if he moves. As you complete the circle and get to the dog's side again, let the leash out so that you end up with the same distance that you started with. During this process give the dog a "Corrective Jerk" accompanied by a firm "No" if he moves. Remember, it is permissible to correct the dog once he has been taught the basics of the command.

How to extend the line. It must be a firm rule that you do not skip from one length to that beyond two feet. The progression must be from six feet to eight, ten, twelve, fourteen, sixteen, eighteen, twenty, twenty-two, twenty-four, twenty-five. Once you start teaching near the end of the clothsline it will become more difficult to execute a Corrective Jerk. However, if you were firm in jerking the dog and saying "No" in the shorter lengths it will not be necessary to jerk the dog very much at that point. Even so, a firm "No" with a jerk executed from a great distance will still do its work. The firmness of your "No" is very important for this command because it will be your only way of correcting the animal once he is off the leash. Hopefully, the dog will have been conditioned to respond to "No" by associating the correction with the Corrective Jerk. A verbal correction should be just as effective as a physical one if you have done your work well.

The ultimate correction. Once you are teaching the dog to "Stay" near the end of the twenty-five-foot line, he may be tempted to break away and run after a bird or some other distraction. The extended distance between you will make him think it is okay. Let the dog run as fast as he wants. Say nothing. Let him get to the end of the rope. Then jerk him hard and walk in the opposite direction as you yell "No" at the top of your voice. This will be a hard correction for the dog and one that he will remember all his life.

The moment of truth. Once the dog has held the position without moving throughout the entire twenty-five feet of line, he is ready to be tested off-leash. It is important to be certain that the animal has performed perfectly up to this point. The off-leash test should be attempted only in a fenced-in area. It is hard to predict if the dog will continue to obey once the line has been removed. If everything has gone well it should make no difference. Remove the leash.

With the dog on your left side, give him the command, "Sit." Then give him the verbal command, "Stay," accompanied by the hand signal. Make the pivotal turn and stand in front of him. Back away slowly until you have reached about twenty-five feet. If the dog has not moved you have our congratulations. Stand and watch him for ten or twenty seconds and return and repeat the procedure.

Many dogs do not remain in position this first time off the leash. It is here that the "throw-chain" is used. If the dog moves or makes a break for it, shout the correction "No" and toss the throw-chain close to him without hitting him. Try to get close enough to place him in "Sit." You will then have to go back to the twenty-five foot line and start again from ten feet, working your way back to the end of the rope.

Alone in a room. One of the more useful applications of "Stay" is when you want the dog to remain in a room while you leave it for a short period of time. Teaching this requires the six-foot leash and the choke collar.

Place the dog in "Sit" and drop the leash to the floor. Using the verbal command and the hand signal place the dog in "Stay." Leave the room. Reenter the room in five seconds. Praise the dog if he did not move. Repeat this ten or fifteen times. Next, extend the length of time that you leave the room. Do it for a ten-second absence. Praise the dog if he did not move and repeat this ten or fifteen times. Keep increasing the time period that you leave the room until you can leave him alone for five minutes. Always let the leash remain connected to the dog's collar even though you are not there to hold it. The leash is a symbol of authority to the dog by this time and it will serve you well.

You may practice this indoor form of "Stay" by putting it to everyday use. Leave the dog alone in a room and have someone ring the doorbell. If the dog runs to the door, give him a Corrective Jerk with an accompanying "No." There are dozens of situations that come up daily in which you can practice "Stay." One way that you can test the dog for "Stay" is by extending the six-foot leash to its fullest length and executing quick, gentle tugs as you command the dog, "Stay," with each tug. If the dog remains in "Stay" even though he is being pulled along, he knows the command very well. Try it.

TEMPERAMENT TIPS

The nervous dog. This kind of dog is very easily distracted. It is important to teach this command in a quiet, private area. A nervous dog in "Stay" is like a dog in a quick-motion film. His head moves from side to side and back and forth. His breathing is very heavy and his body never seems to be still. The best way to teach him "Stay" is by trying to keep his attention. Talk to him in soothing, soft tones in a continuous patter while walking around him. Touch his head gently from time to time to reassure him that he is not being punished and that the session is nothing to fear. Keep the leash taut and high on his neck. Do not choke him. You only want to keep him in place. When walking away from him during the teaching, be sure not to pull on the leash. A nervous dog will respond to it as a signal to move forward. When teaching a nervous dog with the side-to-side technique, do not go completely around any one side. Stop about halfway on one side and go back to center and then walk halfway to the other side. Allow the dog to see your continuous movement so that he won't feel the need to follow you. Be patient when teaching the dog. Try not to confuse nervousness with stubbornness. Only one person should teach the nervous dog this command.

The nervous-shy dog. This command must be taught in private. You must be extremely patient and gentle. Do not jerk the leash at all. Give the commands in a soothing tone of voice. When giving hand signals do not be too quick in your movements as you may scare the dog. Do not raise your voice because the dog may cower. Be gentle and loving at all times. As many members of the family as possible should teach this command. Take as much time as is necessary to teach the shy dog "Sit-Stay." Tender loving care is the key with dogs of this temperament.

The nervous-aggressive dog. This dog can be very difficult to teach because he may try to bite you if you jerk him. Keep the leash high on his neck but do not choke him. When the dog does not respond properly or behaves aggressively, give him a quick jerk upward but then release the collar immediately so as not to choke him. This is very important. Then follow the correction with praise. The command must be taught in private and especially away from other dogs. If the dog is nine months old or older, always be on the alert for a sudden attack. The greatest difficulty in teaching a nervous-aggressive dog is the test of your patience. Do not use any hand signals. Rely on the verbal command and use a soothing tone of voice. Although this will take more time it will be much more effective. Always correct the dog by jerking the leash with both hands. Do not allow the dog to feel threatened by anything when teaching him. Never move quickly. Use slow and confident motions when teaching. This puts the dog at ease and makes him more receptive to the teaching process. If the dog is too difficult you should place him in the care of a professional trainer.

The shy dog. Because you are dealing with a frightened dog, make sure that you do not give loud commands. Patience and affection are your guidelines. The shy dog will be easy to teach because he is usually afraid to move and that condition works well for the command "Stay." Some shy dogs, however, do try to run away. The best way to avoid this is by keeping a taut leash. Use very soothing tones when walking away from or around the dog. This will help keep the animal's attention while giving him confidence at the same time. Teach the dog in a private area with no distractions.

When giving hand signals, execute them very slowly so as not to startle the dog. This is especially important if the dog is hand-shy from being hit. Use your hands affectionately when walking around the dog during that phase of the teaching. This will make him feel safe and secure. "Sit-stay" is one of the best commands for a shy dog. It will help the dog feel confident about training because there are very few corrective Jerks involved. Patience and affection are important in teaching this command to the shy dog.

The stubborn dog. A dog of this temperament will continuously move or get up after being given the command, "Stay." Be very firm in your corrections. Use a private area for teaching and allow no distractions to interrupt the sessions. Once the dog learns the command it should be taught again in an area that offers distractions. If you don't do this, the dog will regress in the training.

One of the problems you will encounter when teaching a stubborn dog "Stay" is that he will follow you as you walk around or away from him. This command should be given firmly as should the corrections. The jerks must be very firm followed by great amounts of praise.

Another problem will be stepping off with your right foot. The moment you step off to move around to face the dog he will quickly jump forward. Keep the leash and collar high on the dog's neck and maintain a taut hold. Once you complete your turn do not move away for ten or even twenty seconds. As you begin to move again maintain a very taut leash so that he will not be able to follow you. If the dog jumps on you or puts his paw on the leash, give him a firm correction followed by praise. Do not allow this to alarm you. You must outlast a stubborn dog and that requires that you do not lose your temper or let him wear away your patience. The Corrective Jerk is the most important training tool when teaching a stubborn dog.

The sedate dog. This is one of the easiest commands in the obedience course for a sedate dog. Only the "Down-Stay" is easier. He will remain in position to the point where you'll think he's already been taught the command. The only way you can be sure that the dog has really learned the command is by doing the following: Give him a gentle jerk and say, "Stay." Repeat this ten or fifteen times in quick succession. If he has learned the command the dog will remain in position. You can even try to pull the dog toward you. If he resists, it can safely be assumed that he knows the command. The command can be taught in any area. Distractions will not bother him. You may have any member of the family teach him this command in addition to yourself. Do not be surprised if the dog zips through each lesson in record time. It has a great deal to do with his sedate temperament.

The aggressive dog. Here again, the training depends on the degree of the animal's aggressiveness. He may simply be a bully or he may be a vicious biter. However, this is the easiest command to teach an aggressive dog no matter how aggressive he is. If the dog starts to growl, curl his lip, or jump at you, give him very hard corrections. The leash and collar should be placed very high on his neck to make the jerks more effective. Teach the dog in a secluded area with no distractions. Always be prepared for an attack. Even though you think you know the dog and feel that he would never bite you, he is quite unpredictable when being taught a command. Leash control is your only defense. One way to deal with him is to keep talking in very soothing tones. Do not pet him and avoid using the hand signal. He may consider your quick hand movements a threat and bite defensively. All commands should be given firmly so as to build his respect for you and the training. If you show any sign of weakness or fear, the dog will take advantage of it and make training nearly impossible.

You must always assume that you may get bitten when training an aggressive dog. This will keep you on your toes and make you demand more respect from the dog. It is only this demand for respect that will get an aggressive dog through obedience training.

13

PUTTING YOUR FRIEND DOWN

("Down" and "Down-Stay")

"DOWN" MEANS...

On command the dog lowers his entire body to the ground or the floor. Although he is completely relaxed, his head remains erect as he looks forward in anticipation of your next command. The dog's front paws are stretched out in front of him forming two parallel straight lines. His rear paws are holding his resting body weight. Some dogs tuck their hind legs in under the body while others extend them both to one side, giving a slight twist to the body. Whichever position is most natural to the dog is acceptable.

FROM THE DOG'S POINT OF VIEW...

This may be the dog's favorite command (especially if he has a sedate temperament). With the exception of those that actually work for a living (police dogs, watchdogs, sheepherders, sled dogs, etc.) most dogs are born loafers and are usually found in some variation of the prone position. They sleep that way, rest that way, watch for vital kitchen activities from the lowest part of the house. Of course, in the summer what is more comfortable than the cool floor or grassy ground under a shade tree? Because most life happens around twenty-four inches off the ground for the average dog, lying down is natural enough. But going down on command is not. The typical dog lowers himself to the floor only if he is tired, bored, or curious. It is usually the last thing that he wants to do when it is most convenient for his owner. Only a dog that is obedience-trained can manage to overcome his desire to nose about and slump to the ground when commanded to do so.

Giving the dog the command, "Down," involves a verbal statement and a hand signal. It is the teaching of the hand signal that can be a problem for some dogs. It is quite possible that you didn't know you weren't supposed to hit your dog, especially with your flattened hands. You couldn't possibly have known that your hands are used only for feeding the dog, patting him affectionately, and *administering hand signals for various commands.* A dog that has been hit by the human hand is going to be *hand-shy* and will be frightened by hand signals. His fright may be expressed by cowering, running, or, quite often, biting. If your dog has been hit you must be careful when teaching him the hand signal for "Down."

Obviously, you must never hit the dog again for your sake as well as his. You will have to reeducate his associations with the human hand. This is possible in most cases where the dog is young. Physical expressions of love such as stroking the animal, food treats, gentle play, brushing, and grooming will all help to change the animal's attitude about hands. If the dog is hand-shy because he has been hit over a long period of time, it may be too late. In that case you must never use hand signals and rely on the verbal command exclusively. No matter what the case may be it is absolutely vital to the success of this course that the animal never be hit again. Your hands must never be used for any form of discipline or punishment. Pointing an accusing finger at the dog is just as harmful, in its way, as hitting him. The hand must never be used for anything negative. The dog does not like it and will not learn anything that way.

"Down" and "Down-Stay" are two extremely useful commands and in the end make the dog happier than the alternatives usually used. When there is cooking going on, guests in the house, perhaps a party, the dog is usually banished to a lonely section of the house or apartment. But a dog that can obey his master and "Stay" in "Down" can remain where all the action is and yet not make a nuisance of himself. It's a wonderful command from the dog's point of view.

HOW TO . . .

"Down" is probably the most difficult command to teach any dog. More time, patience, and, perhaps, tenacity will be required of you to teach this command than for any other. Although dogs like the command once it's been taught, they dislike the teaching process because it is a serious challenge to their free will. Of all the prerogatives the dog is least willing to give up, lying down or standing up are at the top of the list. Mnay a responsive dog has made his last stand on the issue of free will when this command was taught. It can be very difficult or, if you are lucky, very simple. It really depends on the instincts and quirks of the animal. Because so much time and patience are required to teach this command, it is one that is better learned and best performed by the dog than any other. "Down" and "Down-Stay" will also be used by you more than any other command during the course of any single day in the dog's life.

Because this command is so tricky to teach, a more individualized approach is necessary in terms of techniques used. For that reason we offer five different techniques to choose from and explain quite specifically which temperament of dog should be taught with which individual technique. Having five ways to choose from also gives more than enough alternatives if one does not work for your dog. This is, then, in effect, a teaching primer for the command "Down."

1. PAW TECHNIQUE (STANDING AT THE DOG'S SIDE AND THEN IN FRONT OF HIM)

This technique is the standard one and is best for dogs of the following temperaments: responsive, nervous, nervous-shy, shy, sedate, and stubborn. *Never use this technique for the nervous-aggressive dog or the aggressive dog.* It is very important that you procede from technique number one (Paw) to technique number two (Hand). This is the technique that teaches the dog to respond to the "Down" hand signal.

At the dog's side. Begin by placing the dog in "Sit-Stay" and stand by his side so that he is on your left. You and the dog should now be facing in the same direction. Hold the leash with either hand. Lower your body so that you kneel on one knee (whichever is most comfortable). Gently grab the dog's two front paws with your free hand. Place your middle finger between the two paws so that they do not get pressed painfully together (see Figure 10). Give the dog the verbal command, "Down," in your teaching tone of voice. As you give the verbal command pull the dog's front paws ahead of him. This takes away his main support, which makes him gently fall into the "Down" position. The dog has no choice. Repeat this action fifteen times or until he goes down with almost no resistance at all.

Leash control. It is quite possible that the dog will attempt to get up and leave the teaching area once he decides he doesn't like what's being taught. The leash is your only means of controlling the situation and continuing the lesson. Do not administer any Corrective Jerks at this stage. Simply hold the dog in place with the leash extended above his head and keep it taut. In a situation like this, use a soothing tone of voice and give the dog a great deal of praise each and every step of the way.

Sometimes a playful dog will roll over on his side after being pulled down by his paws. Although this is bad form for the command, to be sure, it is not important at this time. Praise the dog anyway because he did the important thing, he went down on command (even though he was forced to do so). This kind of dog may even try to romp and play once he has gone down. Do not reprimand him at this stage. It can be corrected later once the dog has gotten used to obeying the command. Of course, it isn't a good idea to encourage any playful activity during the lesson, either. Simply use the leash to guide the dog back into the "Sit-Stay" and repeat the teaching procedure.

The proper way to say "Down." The verbal command, "Down," is not said in the same manner as the other verbal commands. The very word itself and its unique delivery are teaching aids and help the dog to understand what you want. If the word is distorted by elongating the middle vowel it takes you longer to say the word. By stretching the length of time to complete the word, you can actually lower the tone of your voice in the middle of saying "Down" and thus indicate to the dog that he must, in turn, lower his body. It does not take the dog very long to make this most useful association. The combination of the word and the elongated middle sound that descends in tone will make a lifetime impression and help the animal to more readily obey the command.

Pulling his paws as you stand in front of him. Because you will eventually be giving the command, "Down," to the dog from a great distance, it is important that he get used to obeying you from his front view.

Place the dog in "Sit-Stay" and stand next to him so that he is by your left side. Starting off with the right foot, pivot around so that you and the animal are staring at each other, face to face. Lower your body so that you kneel on one knee (whichever is most comfortable). Holding the leash with one hand grab the dog's two front paws with the free hand. Be certain that you separate the two paws with your middle finger to avoid hurting him. Give the verbal command in the elongated descending tone, "Down." Pull the dog's front paws ahead of him as you give the verbal command. The dog will gently fall into the "Down" position.

Holding the leash may prove to be a bit clumsy during this procedure. It must be held twelve to eighteen inches above the dog's head and it must be taut. Naturally, the leash must be adjusted in length as the dog moves from "Sit" to "Down." Leash control can be critical during this aspect of the command. At any point the dog may start to move forward, thinking you are going to "Heel" with him. Some dogs will come toward you simply because you are facing them and they think the lesson is over. In either case they must be kept in place with a taut leash rather than a correction. Although this technique will probably be learned quickly, reinforce the dog's un- derstanding of it by repeating the procedure fifteen times. You are

Figure 10. Poodle-Labrador mix, *Sir Gregory*, enjoys the attention as trainer shows "Paw Technique" for teaching "Down." Index finger separates the two paws so they do not squeeze painfully together.

now ready to proceed to the second method, the Hand Technique. Here you will learn to give the proper hand signal.

2. HAND TECHNIQUE (STANDING AT THE DOG'S SIDE AND THEN IN FRONT OF HIM)

This method of teaching "Down" is never used by itself. One of the other techniques must always be taught first before moving on to this one. The only exception to this rule is in teaching the sedate dog. Dogs of this temperament should be trained by the hand technique alone, and no other.

The Hand Technique is good for dogs of the following temperaments: responsive, nervous, nervous-shy, shy, sedate, and stubborn. *It should never be used for aggressive dogs and some nervous-aggressive dogs.*

By the dog's side. The purpose of this technique is to teach the dog the proper hand signal for going into the "Down" position. We emphasize teaching this technique by the dog's side first for reasons of safety. If your dog is hand-shy because he has been hit, or because of a personality quirk doesn't like human hands approaching his face, he may bite. However, introducing hand movements from the side helps to assure him that no harm is meant.

This phase of the teaching is going to be hard on the dog and for this reason you must soothe him with your voice and remain in a cheerful frame of mind. Do not be harsh, authoritative, or anything but light in manner.

Place the dog in "Sit-Stay" on your left side. Both dog and master are facing in the same direction. Kneel on the ground on one knee (whichever is most comfortable) while holding the leash with the *right* hand. The leash should extend from the dog's collar across the width of your body to your right hand. Do not allow any slack in the leash. Do not allow the dog to move or play. This can be achieved with a tightening of the leash. If the dog moves, give him the command, "Sit," and then praise him.

Now comes the most important part of this technique. Flatten your left hand and close all the fingers together. They should be in a

Figure 11. Teaching the dog "Down" by using the "Hand Technique" while kneeling to the side of the animal. The flat of the hand, palm down, lands on top of the leash and exerts enough pressure to force the dog to the ground.

Figure 12. Teaching the dog "Down" by using the "Hand Technique" while kneeling *in front* of the animal.

straight line with the fingertips forward and the palm side facing the ground. Raise your left hand so that it is somewhat above the eye level of the dog and to the right of his head. Make sure there is no slack in the leash.

Simultaneously, give the verbal command, "Down," as suggested in technique number one, and lower your left hand toward the ground. In doing so, the flat of your palm will hit the top of the leash about where the clip connects to the choke collar (see Figure 11). As your hand presses against the leash it will push both leash and dog to the ground. Through his peripheral vision the dog can see your left hand push him into the "Down" position. The result is his association of your descending left hand with the command for him to lower his body to the ground. This is how he learns to respond to the proper hand signal. Eventually, you will be able to lower your left arm (hand flattened as described above) from a great distance and the dog will go into the "Down" position without any verbal command at all.

Repeat this procedure at least fifteen times or as many times as necessary to make the dog go down without any resistance. Some dogs resist this part of the training and offer opposition. It is a matter of whose will is going to prevail. We suggest that you force the issue and just keep pushing him down until he offers no more opposition. His choke collar will tighten around his neck but will certainly loosen when the dog is completely down. If the opposition becomes an impossible struggle you should stop the lesson, praise him, review one or two earlier commands, and then begin "Down" over again from the beginning. Be patient and understand that this is harder on the dog than it is on you. Lavish the dog with praise and be aware that this is hard work for him. He is going to be very tired after this lesson and it is a good idea to let him have as much rest as he needs. He'll tell you when he's ready to play or learn again.

Hand technique from the front of the dog. Once the dog allows himself to be pushed into "Down" by your hand from the side, it is safe to assume that you can do it from the front. This is an important step in reinforcing his knowledge of the hand signal. If all went well the dog will understand that your descending hand is not going to hit him or hurt him in any way. He should be able to tolerate it from his front view.

Once again, place the dog in "Sit-Stay" and step in front of him by starting off on your right foot. As you and the dog face each other, hold the leash with your *left* hand. Kneel on one knee and repeat the action described on page 160. With the right hand extended upward, fingers close together, push the top of the leash downward as your arm descends (see Figure 12). This is to be accompanied by the verbal command , "Down." As your voice elongates and descends in tone the dog is actually pushed to the ground by your right hand on top of the leash. Fifteen repetitions are requisite here or as many more as necessary. By now nothing short of good form is tolerable. The dog may not nip at your fingers, roll over, or hide between your legs once he has assumed the "Down" position. Whenever the dog breaks discipline place him in "Sit-Stay" and begin the procedure again.

From the front while standing straight. Before beginning this next step, review everything the dog has learned in the first two steps. That accomplished, you are now ready to proceed to the next objective, which is to hand-signal the dog into "Down" without kneeling.

Place the dog in "Sit-Stay" and get in front of him. Stand one or two feet away. Hold the leash with your left hand and tighten it above the dog's head if he tries to move away. This will always force the dog to remain in the "Sit" position. Remember, you cannot give the animal a correction because he is still in the learning process.

If you are standing two feet away from the dog, allow an extra foot of leash to hang as slack. Raise your right arm straight up with the fingers close together (this is the correct position just before giving the hand signal). Give the dog the verbal command, "Down," using the elongated and descending tone of voice. Begin to lower your right arm as you say the verbal command. Allow the flattened right hand, palm down, to land on the top of the leash. The dog's reaction should be to go into the "Down" position without having to be forced with physical pressure. Praise the dog lavishly and repeat this procedure fifteen times.

Extending the distance. This is a crucial phase because your hand will not touch the leash as it is lowered. Place the dog in "Sit-Stay" and stand three or three and a half feet in front of him. Because the

1

2

Figure 13. The hand signal for the command, "Down."

3

4

dog now knows the basics of this command it is permissible to administer a Corrective Jerk if he fails to obey or tries to move out of position. Three feet is still close enough to accomplish this.

Raise your right arm straight up as you maintain a flattened hand with fingers close together. Give the verbal command, "Down," and slowly lower your arm. Make the rhythm of your arm's movement coincide with the verbal command. You should not stop saying "Down" until your arm has completed its movement. The arm comes down, palm downward, heading for the leash. *This time your hand misses the leash, moves past it and continues to your side.* You have just executed the hand signal as it will always look (see Figure 13). The arm simply moves downward toward its original position at the side of the body. The dog has anticipated being forced into "Down" and should go into proper position without force or pressure. Repeat this procedure fifteen times or until the dog is obeying the command perfectly. It will not be long before the dog, with practice, will be able to go into the proper position with only the verbal command or only the hand signal. Test the dog by practicing the verbal command alone. Next, use the hand signal only. This has been very difficult for your dog and therefore he deserves your praise and admiration every step of the way.

3. THE BELLY TECHNIQUE
(FROM THE DOG'S SIDE ONLY)

This technique is optional and is recommended for dogs who have the following temperaments: nervous, nervous-shy, shy, sedate, and stubborn.

Place the dog in "Sit-Stay" as you stand at his side. In this technique you are turned in, facing the side of the animal. Kneel on the ground on one knee and hold the leash with your left hand. Place your right hand under the dog's belly as though you were going to hold it. Give the verbal command, "Down." At the same time, place your left hand on the dog's back, holding him in place; your right hand slides forward, under his belly, pushing the dog's paws forward so that he gently falls into the "Down" position. You are almost lifting his front paws off the ground and pushing them forward (see Figure 14). Keep extending your right hand forward so the dog is forced to go into the proper position.

4. The Foot-Leash Technique (standing at the dog's side and then in front of him)

This technique should be used only on dogs of the following temperaments: stubborn, nervous-aggressive, and aggressive. When dealing with dogs that require this technique, the hand signal should not be attempted. The Foot-Leash Technique must *never* be used on shy, nervous-shy, or sedate dogs. This method is also useful for oversized dogs.

With the dog on your left side place him in "Sit-Stay" while holding the leash with both hands. Allow only a small amount of slack in the leash. Give the dog the verbal command, "Down," with the elongated, descending tone of voice. At the same time raise your left foot high off the ground and set it on top of the leash where the leash clip connects to the choke collar. As your voice goes down in tone apply pressure to the leash with your left foot. Obviously, this will force the dog into the "Down" position. The trick is to pull up on the leash as you press your foot down, allowing the leash to slip around your shoe (see Figure 15). Give the animal lavish praise when he reaches the ground. This technique is often necessary for stubborn dogs that refuse to learn any other way. It certainly is the only answer if the stubborn dog is also very large and powerful. Repeat this procedure fifteen times. After you are sure the dog is responding with a minimum of resistance, repeat the technique from the front, while facing the dog. Do not attempt to teach the animal the hand signal. In a short time, after much practice, the dog will go into the proper position with the verbal command only.

A word of caution: It is harmful to pull up on the leash too quickly and will only cause the animal to resist with all his strength. If you are too harsh with this technique you can hurt the dog. When using this method, be careful if the dog growls or attempts to bite. If the struggle is too great you may try technique number five.

Figure 14. Teaching "Down" with the "Belly Technique." With the left hand on the dog's back, slide the right hand forward, under the dog's belly. The animal's paws are forced forward so that he gently falls into the "Down" position.

Figure 15. Another method for teaching "Down" is the "Foot-Leash Technique." This method is useful for dogs with stubborn, nervous-aggressive, or aggressive temperaments. It can also be used for over-sized dogs.

5. THE SLIDING-LEASH TECHNIQUE (STANDING AT THE DOG'S SIDE AND THEN IN FRONT OF HIM)

This technique should only be used on dogs of the following temperaments: stubborn, nervous-aggressive, and aggressive. *Never* use it on shy, nervous-shy, sedate, or nervous dogs. Do not attempt to teach the hand signal (technique number two) when resorting to this one.

With the dog on your left side place him in "Sit-Stay." Hold the leash with both hands. Allow just enough slack so that part of the leash touches the ground. Place your left shoe on top of the leash so that it is located in the space between the heel and sole. Give the dog the verbal command, "Down," in the elongated, descending tone of voice. At the same time pull up on the leash with all your strength in one smooth, continuous hoist, allowing the leash to slide through the arch of your shoe. This will result in the dog's being forced to move into the "Down" position (see Figure 16). Praise the dog when he reaches the ground. Repeat this fifteen times or until the dog performs properly, without resistance. Next, move to the front of the dog, facing him, and repeat the procedure in the same manner. Do not hurt the animal with harsh or overly zealous tugs of the leash. If you still cannot make the dog perform properly, it may be well to skip this command or consult a professional trainer.

TEMPERAMENT TIPS

The nervous dog. "Down" is the hardest command to teach. It requires great patience. It will be difficult for a nervous dog to sit still when you attempt to teach him "Down." Maintain firm leash control. If the animal is not too fragile and he keeps jumping out of the "Sit-Stay," try technique number five (the sliding leash technique). Work slowly with a nervous dog. If he resists too vigorously, stop work and try again five minutes later. This command can make a nervous dog more nervous if you do not take the amount of time necessary for his shaky temperament. Teach the command in a secluded area with no one present but the one trainer. Break up the lessons as much as possible. Give him two or three a day over one or two weeks' time.

The nervous-shy dog. This command should be taught by one trainer only and in a quiet area. The best technique for dogs of this temperament is the Belly Technique (number three). It works well because of the closeness involved. For the same reason the Paw Technique (number one) is also good. Never use any of the foot techniques on a nervous-shy dog. It will scare the dog and negate the training. Your soothing tone of voice is especially important with this temperament. He needs assurance and a great deal of praise. Do not use the word "No" in a harsh tone, and avoid jerking the dog. This command will take a longer time to teach than usual. Two or three lessons a day (five minutes each) should be given over a one- or two-week period. If the dog is hand-shy, concentrate on verbal commands only. Using your hands will only frighten the animal and make the command more difficult to teach. You will have to use your judgment on whether to teach the hand signal or not.

The nervous-aggressive dog. It is easy to get bitten by this type of dog if extreme caution is not exercised. Try teaching the Paw Technique (number one), but from the side only. If the dog growls ferociously or curls his lip, give him hard corrections and see if he responds well after that. If he keeps responding with threatening gestures, stop the Paw Technique completely. Your body is very close to the dog, making you vulnerable to being bitten. This is especially dangerous if the animal is nine months old or older. Resort to the Sliding-Leash Technique (number five). The dog will still try to fight you but he will not understand where the source of pressure is coming from. He will be too confused to attack anything. The dog will probably respond very well to this technique if you use a firm but soothing tone of voice. The Foot-Leash Technique (number four) is also a useful alternative. It is important to keep talking to the dog as you push him to the ground with your foot on the leash. Do not teach this type of dog the hand signal and use a private area with no distractions for training purposes. Give the dog two or three lessons a day for one or two weeks. Each lesson should not be more than five minutes long. The following factors must be considered when

Figure 16. The "Sliding-Leash Technique."

teaching the nervous-aggressive dog the "Down" command: praise, encouragement, patience, and *caution.*

The shy dog. Allow no distractions when teaching this type of dog and do not have more than one trainer conducting the lessons. Be very loving and patient. You may use only the Paw Technique (number one) or the Belly Technique (number three). Never use the foot techniques. You may teach the hand signal (number two) if the dog is not hand-shy. If the dog puts up a fight when being taught this command, stop the lesson and wait five minutes before attempting it again. The lessons should be short (five minutes) and give two or three a day for one to two weeks. Be patient and never use too firm a tone of voice. The dog can be made to feel secure during the teaching process by stroking him with your hands, using a soft tone of voice when giving the command, avoiding a taut leash, and by not administering any Corrective Jerks.

The stubborn dog. All techniques can be used (techniques one through five), depending on which works best on your particular dog. The dog may resist the Paw Technique. If he does, do not be too harsh. Do not confuse the dog's stubbornness with an inability to learn. If the dog mouths your hand during the teaching process give him a firm "No," a gentle Corrective Jerk, and begin the Paw Technique again from the beginning. In teaching the stubborn dog the Belly Technique, the trick is to execute the sliding motion quickly so that the dog does not have time to react. When learning the Sliding-Leash Technique (number five), the dog may offer a great deal of resistance, to the point of choking himself. Relax the training when this happens. Stop for five minutes and begin again. The greatest problem when teaching a stubborn dog the command, "Down," is letting the animal get the best of you. Go slowly and patiently and do not be too eager for instant results. It is possible to worsen the dog's temperament by pushing too hard, too fast. Be firm but not harsh. The hand signal can be taught to the stubborn dog but only one person should do the teaching.

The sedate dog. This dog can be taught by more than one person and distractions are not a problem. Techniques one, two, and three (Paw, Hand, and Belly) can be used to teach the sedate dog the

Figure 17. Professional trainers stand with *Herschel*, *Sir Gregory*, and *Butch* in "Down-Stay."

command "Down." One of the things you can anticipate when bringing the animal "Down" is that he will roll over on his back or indulge in playful activities. Do not scold the dog for doing so. And do not assume that the dog has learned the command simply because he goes down quickly. Don't forget, sedate dogs are, for the most part, lethargic. Just keep repeating the teaching process until you are sure he knows it. Use the leash to keep the dog in the proper "Down" position without rolling over or moving away. Make the dog remain in position for one or two minutes so that he understands what you expect of him.

The aggressive dog. The two foot techniques (four and five) are the only ones recommended for a truly aggressive dog. You must be careful to avoid being bitten. When teaching the Sliding-Leash Technique, keep repeating the command and pull up on the leash very slowly as you talk to the dog in soft tones. If the dog behaves aggressively toward you, give him one or two very hard Corrective Jerks. It may even be necessary to suspend him off the ground with the leash. "Down" is a very difficult command to teach a very aggressive animal. You may have to avoid this command or consult a professional trainer. If you are going to try it, use a private area with no distractions. No more than one trainer should teach this type of dog so difficult a command. Five or six lessons a day (five minutes each) are in order, and spend three to four weeks teaching the command. Be certain you can handle your dog before teaching this command. It can be dangerous, depending on the degree of aggressiveness of the dog.

"DOWN-STAY" MEANS . . .

The dog has assumed the "Down" position on the ground or floor and remains there, on command, until he is released by verbal command (see Figure 17).

HOW TO . . .

"Down-Stay" is quite similar to "Sit-Stay" and the teaching technique is almost the same. Do not use the animal's name when giving the verbal command, "Stay." Place the dog in "Down" and give him the command, "Stay." As you give the verbal command place your flattened hand (fingers close together) four inches in front of the dog's eyes. This is the hand signal for "Stay" and always accompanies the verbal command. You must temporarily block the dog's vision for an instant and then quickly remove your hand. If the dog has already been taught "Sit-Stay," it is a foregone conclusion that he knows "Down-Stay." "Stay" in the "Down" position may confuse some dogs and they will need more lessons. In that event go back to Chapter 12, and go over the material once again.

14

A DOG ALSO RISES
("Come When Called")

"COME WHEN CALLED" MEANS . . .

The master uses a precise verbal command and a hand signal so that the dog stops what he is doing, runs to the one who has called him, and places himself in a "Sit" position when he reaches his destination.

FROM THE DOG'S POINT OF VIEW . . .

If the dog has been properly motivated with lavish praise, he is going to enjoy being called by his owner. If not, this command is going to be a royal pain in the haunch and the animal is going to be unreliable when called. Sometimes he'll come and sometimes he won't. It will all depend on his mood and other interests. That's how it is with this most demanding of commands.

"Come When Called" is used in two environments. It is used indoors where conditions are safe, controlled, and free of any hazard for the dog if he fails to obey. The other environment is outdoors where the exact opposite set of conditions exist. It is an important fact that *"Come When Called" cannot be taught outdoors, off-leash, if the dog is one year old or older.* Not only is it too dangerous but it is well-nigh impossible to get a mature dog to resist his need and/or desire to roam about as he pleases when allowed off-leash. A mature dog does not realize his dependency as does a puppy and cannot be conditioned to resist chasing other animals or, as in the case of hunting breeds, moving objects. If the dog has any amount of hunting breed in him he can only be taught this command outdoors if he is a puppy and if the trainer is absolutely diligent and very hard-working.

Because most dogs spend the greater part of their lives indoors and because they all have some wildness about them, the out-of-doors is pure, delicious excitement. Even though he is on a leash the average dog jumps with joy at the prospect of a simple walk outside the house. Imagine his sense of pleasure at being sent outside without any restraint. It's not that he won't come back eventually (although some will not) that is the problem. The frustration lies in *when* the dog returns and if he does so on command. In most cases the answer is no to the latter and whenever he feels like it to the former.

Before deciding to teach your dog this command off-leash and outdoors, it is important to understand that the dog may someday make a dash for an animal across the road or street and get hit by an automobile. Letting a dog loose outdoors is very risky and some of the best-disciplined dogs have on occasion failed to respond to "Come When Called." But even so, the command is still extremely useful indoors and is well worth the teaching effort. It is very impressive to watch a well-disciplined dog run to his master when called and place himself in "Sit." Being able to maneuver the animal around inside the house has great advantages that will become apparent as the command is used.

From a dog's point of view his behavior develops from a built-in sense of logic and, if we may go so far, fairness. There is nothing worse for him than responding to your call only to be yelled at or punished. He obeyed you cheerfully and was then rewarded with an unpleasant experience. The only possible result of this unfortunate behavior is that the dog will sooner or later stop coming when he is called. It would be stupid for man or beast to lumber up to someone who whacked him on the snout for responding, and then to slurp him on the face. The point here is clear. *Never call a dog to you and then express a negative feeling, word, or action.* The most common mistake made by dog owners is to call their dogs to them in order to confront them with something bad that they did. First of all it is futile because a dog cannot associate your wrath with his wrongdoing sixty seconds after he has done it. Second, you will be teaching him not to obey the command "Come When Called." *For the same reasons you must never use the dog's name for anything negative.* Using the dog's name or the command "Come When Called" for the purpose of correction will create a bad association with either of these valuable training tools and will be like throwing them away.

If your dog needs to be corrected for anything at all, especially if he disobeys a command, it is vital that *you go to him to administer it.* Success in this command depends on the dog's confidence that something pleasant is the result of his obedience. Unreserved praise is the only way to achieve this attitude in him. Praise him each and every time he obeys, and praise him well.

HOW TO . . .

An important goal to work for when teaching this command is to have the dog obey you immediately. Do not allow him to hesitate so that a second command becomes necessary. There may be a time when his immediate response will save his life.

This command begins with *on-leash* work. The dog will never learn the *off-leash* portion if he doesn't learn the on-leash part to perfection first. This requires a group of sessions during which the length of the leash (and clothesline) increases in distance. *Do not work with the dog off-leash until he is absolutely perfect on-leash.*

ON-LEASH

It does not matter if you begin teaching this command indoors or out. You will need only the six-foot leash and a choke collar. (When working with the dog *off-leash* [see page 181], you will need a fifty-foot length of clothesline. Before beginning your first lesson, brush the dog up on all the commands he has learned up to this point. This will help get the dog in the proper frame of mind for this difficult command.

Begin by putting the dog in the "Sit" position. Stand directly in front of the dog, about five and a half feet away. Hold the leash with your left hand, allowing just a little slack so that the dog will not accidentally be pulled toward you. If the leash is pulled at all, the dog will leave his position. Hold the leash slightly above your waist. This will give you optimum control over the animal.

The lesson begins with the verbal command, which must be given with great joy and enthusiasm. The sound of your voice should tell the dog that a fun thing is about to happen. Naturally, the fun thing will be the great praise you will give him for obeying properly. "Come When Called" is an action command and, therefore, requires the dog's name to be prefixed to the command, "Come." In this case, however, you must use a prefix to the prefix. Use the word "Okay" before saying the dog's name. The entire verbal command is *"Okay, Yuban, come!"* The reason we use "Okay" before the name is to insure an upbeat sound. From a distance the command, "Blockhead, come!" might sound like punishment or correction because you had to raise your voice. "Okay," said in a high-pitched and happy tone of voice, makes it clear to the dog that only good things are involved. This word is difficult to say in a negative manner. Since the Chapter 8, "Verbal Tolls", the dog should have a pleasant association with the word.

When saying the full command, it is important to emphasize the word "Okay." Eliminate any harshness from your voice and make it sound as affectionate as possible. Once the dog learns the command he should start moving toward you when he hears "Okay," as it dominates the whole phrase. *"Okay, Snoopy, come!"* Take a vow that this is the only way you will ever call the dog to you from now on. Make it clear to all members of the family and work hard to be consistent. It is very important. Try calling the dog in this manner and see if he comes to you. If he does give him lavish praise. If he doesn't *do not* correct him. Keep calling the dog with the verbal command until he finally does come to you. It may take a short while.

Gently pull the leash. Now that the dog at least moves toward you on the verbal command it is time to reinforce his understanding. Give the verbal command and on the word "Okay," gently pull the leash. This is how it works: "Okay, [Gently pull the leash.] Lucretia, come." (She comes to you.) "Good girl. What a good girl." Never forget the praise. The quality of the dog's learning will depend on the quality of your praise. Do not be inhibited. Once you are outdoors and working for longer distances you are going to have to compete with children's laughter, stray dogs, birds, and anything else that moves or makes noise. Praise will win out over all of it.

Teaching the hand signal. The verbal command is always accompanied by a hand signal. The hand signal helps eliminate any confusion for the dog if he is called from a great distance. The hand signal is based on the very common gesture that is used to summon a human being from a long way off. The right arm leaves its hanging position at the side of the body and is raised in a turning, leftward motion as though it were wrapping around a large object. The entire command for the purposes of this lesson goes like this: "Okay, [Pull the leash with your left hand. Raise your right arm and swing it around to your left side. Complete the gesture and return it to its natural position.] Morris, come." Praise the dog.

The "Sit" position. Start by placing the dog in "Sit-Stay" and stand in front of him at a distance of almost six feet. Give the verbal command, "Okay, [Give the hand signal. Pull the leash.] Strudwick, come!" Immediately start pulling the leash toward you like a fishing line, using a hand-over-hand method. Do this until the line is mostly taken up. As the dog gets to your feet give him the command, "Sit," and raise twelve inches of leash above his head tautly so that he has no choice but to obey (see Figure 18). Heap tons of praise on him so that he begins to do it on his own, if only to be praised.

Having the dog go into the "Sit" position after he "Comes When Called" is done for reasons other than show. If the dog is some distance away, he responds to your command by running. If he has enough distance he can build up his speed to approximately thirty miles per hour or more. If he crashes into you it will knock you down. Or, he may not be able to stop and will run past you. Once he has been taught to "Sit" after responding to "Come" he will automatically pace himself so that he begins to slow down before he gets to you. All of the above techniques should be repeated at least fifteen times each, or until the dog performs properly. For safety reasons you must use the leash at all times. Once the dog is doing all this properly you may increase the distance for him to travel by backing away as he walks toward you. Use verbal praise as you back away.

OFF-LEASH

A great deal of time is necessary to teach your dog "Come When Called" outdoors, off-leash. Perhaps several months, depending on the animal's rate of learning and your availability to conduct the necessary sessions. We do not recommend that dogs living in the city be taught this command under the above-described circumstances. The exception to this would be those living in a fenced area or near a closed-off park or field. Once again we must state that it will be difficult to teach this command, off-leash, to a dog one year old or older.

Get a fifty-foot clothesline. Assuming that the dog has learned "Come When Called" on the six-foot leash, it is time to teach him from a distance of ten feet. Attach the clothesline to the dog's leash. From ten feet and on you are going to have less control because your Corrective Jerks will not be as effective from this distance. Even so, you will still have the dog under some control.

The procedure is the same as the on-leash method except that you will be standing in front of the dog at a distance of ten feet. Give the dog the verbal command accompanied by the hand signal. Pull the line in toward you using the hand-over-hand method. Once the dog gets to your feet, give him the command, "Sit," and hold the leash tautly, twelve inches above his head. Lavish the dog with praise. Repeat this fifteen times or until the dog performs without leash guidance.

When he starts obeying correctly at ten feet, go back to the six-foot distance and repeat the procedure. When the dog accomplishes that, try the ten-foot distance again. Repeating the

1

2

3

4

Figure 18. Director of Training for the National Institute of Dog Training, Inc., Bruce Renick, teaches willing pupil "Come When Called." Give the verbal command, "Okay, Connie, come." Give the hand signal (photo 2), pull the leash toward you. As the dog gets to your feet give him the command, "Sit." Raise the leash above his head tautly. Praise him.

5

various distances will reinforce the dog's understanding of the command so that he will never forget it.

Extending the leash in five-foot increments. After repeating the command from ten feet (assuming the dog obeys properly), it is time to move to fifteen feet. It will be clumsy trying to reel the line in from this distance. The dog will probably arrive at your feet before it all can be pulled in. But if the dog is coming to you on command and then sitting, the taut leash will not be necessary. If the dog does not perform properly, you must begin working at six feet again so that you do have taut leash control. If the dog does what he is supposed to at ten feet, he will do the same at fifteen, twenty, twenty-five, thirty, thirty-five, forty, forty-five, and on to the full fifty feet. Simply keep repeating the training as described for the six-foot distance for each extended five feet. Repeat the procedure fifteen times for each distance and then return to the six-foot distance as a refresher.

Long-distance corrections. Obviously, the point to keeping the dog tied to the clothesline is that you will be able to maintain control as he proceeds from distance to distance. If nothing else it will prevent him from running away. The line permits you to exercise some control while the dog is moving toward you in the middle of the command. If something distracts the animal and he makes a break, you are still in a position to make a correction. Allow the dog to run to the end of the line. As he does hold on tightly so that he is jarred at the instant of impact. In a loud voice yell, "No!" It is a rough correction, but one that he will remember for his entire life. Remember, once he is allowed off the leash his life will depend on how well you have trained him. The clothesline, though clumsy, still gives you the ability to correct the dog from a great distance and that is a large advantage. Chances are that this will happen several times during these lessons.

The moment of truth. It is important that the dog prove his ability to obey "Come When Called" properly from six feet to fifty feet before you try him off-leash. If this has been accomplished you are ready for the big moment. The big chance you take is whether he will make any distinction between obeying on-leash and off-leash. Please work in an enclosed area. The dog may assume that he has to obey only if the leash is on. In that case he will make a run for the thing of greatest interest to him, not caring that you are about to go into cardiac arrest. If this happens try not to panic. The worst thing you can do is run after the dog. It only makes the dog run farther away from you. Surprisingly, you must run in the opposite direction, encouraging the dog to play with you. The dog will follow if he thinks it's a game. You must talk to him cheerfully if you want him to get within reach. Once he does, praise him! As much as you may want to holler or hit the dog, resist the temptation and praise him. If the game doesn't work and the dog still has not returned, then you must get down on your knees and playfully attract the dog with encouraging words. If the dog is close enough, give him the verbal command, "Sit," and then, "Stay." However you manage to get the dog under control, be sure to praise him for finally obeying you. This is crucial. You must never correct the dog once he returns to you or he will never return again.

If after working up to fifty feet of line the dog fails the off-leash command, use your throw-chain as a correction. You may have no choice but to start over again from six feet. No doubt you will move from distance to distance much faster than originally. If the dog now fails to obey the command, he may be corrected with the Corrective Jerk accompanied by a firm "No." Do not forget to praise the dog for correcting himself. Once you get back to the fifty-foot distance and are ready to try him off-leash again, make sure you are in a secluded area with no distractions. Be very firm and maintain a no-nonsense attitude. Repeat the entire procedure until he finally comes to you from fifty feet without a leash. Once the dog responds properly you may try him in an area that offers distractions.

Temperament Tips

The nervous dog. After the dog has been placed in "Sit-Stay" and is waiting for the first command of the lesson, he will probably be restless and edgy. The dog will keep turning around and not pay attention to you. For this reason you should select a private, secluded area with no distractions. Begin this command inside your home.

Only one person should train the dog. Hand signals at this stage of the training will be a waste of time. After you have given the dog the command, "Come," he may not walk to you on a straight line because of his nervousness. In that case pull the leash to you rather quickly and guide him into the proper "Sit" position. When you pull the leash he may resist, bite the leash, claw it, or mouth it. Be prepared for this and stop it by administering a quick, mild jerk accompanied by a firm "No." Release the leash and repeat the command. Limit all lessons to five or ten minutes and give two or three a day. Do not lose your patience if the dog moves out of "Stay" before you give the "Come" command. Put him back in the proper position and start again. Do not correct the dog if he jumps on you after obeying the initial command. Guide him into the "Sit" position and keep doing it that way until he gets the idea. The nervous dog should never be trained off-leash because he can never be relied upon to come when called.

The nervous-shy dog. This command must be taught alone in an area with no distractions. The dog may try to run away or run toward you before you get a chance to teach him anything. The best way to cope with this is to review "Sit-Stay" with the dog and make sure he knows it very well before teaching him "Come." Do not use the hand signal if the dog is hand-shy because he may confuse it with being hit. Give him two or three lessons a day (five minutes each). The best place to start teaching this command is in your home. He will be much more trusting and will consequently learn faster. In the beginning do not ask the dog to "Sit" when he comes to you. That can be taught later after he is comfortable with the idea of coming. The objective is to build up the dog's confidence in you and the command you are trying to teach him. Praise is your best tool. Do not train this type of dog off-leash.

The nervous-aggressive dog. One trainer should teach this type of dog, alone, in an area with no distractions. Begin in your own home. When you begin teaching this command, the dog may fight the leash by biting it, clawing it, and snarling and growling. He may also leap up in the air as though he is having a fit. Do not jerk the dog hard or he may try to jump at you. Use soft, soothing tones and much encouragement. Once the dog starts coming to you, do not command him to "Sit." Let him get used to moving toward you first. You may teach him to "Sit" at a later time. If the dog does jump at you or becomes very aggressive, give him a hard Corrective Jerk accompanied by a firm "No." Put him in "Sit-Stay" and repeat the original command. Use verbal commands only. Never use hand signals with a nervous-aggressive dog. If he was ever hit (chances are he was) he may react viciously to a hand signal. Never trust dogs of this temperament off the leash.

The shy dog. Begin instruction for this command in your own home and do not allow any distractions such as other members of the family. Give all commands in a soft tone of voice and be very gentle. Work the leash gently, especially when pulling the dog toward you. Lavish him with praise when he does start coming to you. If the dog offers resistance by digging in with his paws on the floor, bend down, coax him with soothing words. If you conduct the lessons outside do not use the hard sidewalk. Teach this command on a soft, grassy area so there is no possibility of the dog's hurting his tender pads. This command takes an enormous amount of time and patience for the shy dog. The shy dog may crawl to you on his belly or roll on his back when given the command, "Come." Be patient and keep calling him. If he comes to you and tries to crawl between your legs, do not correct him. The same applies if he jumps on you out of fear. The most important part in the beginning is that he comes to you. How he comes to you or if he "Sits" can always be corrected later. Never say "No" to the shy dog and never jerk him. This will only reinforce his fear so he may refuse ever to respond properly to the command. Do not use the hand signal. He may be hand-shy without your knowing it. Never trust him off-leash. It's the easiest way for him to get killed by an automobile.

The stubborn dog. Teach this dog in an area with no distractions. However, more than one member of the family may attend the sessions for the purpose of learning about the command. More than one person may train the dog. The stubborn dog is definitely going to fight the leash when given this command. If you work outside use a grassy area so as not to hurt the dog's sensitive pads. The dog may jump and twist his paws in the leash to hold it down, or he may jump at you when this command is first given. The dog may resist by backing away in an attempt to pull the leash out of your hand. Be firm in your command and make sure he sits in front of you correctly the first time. If you give this type of dog the opportunity, he will take advantage of you. Use both verbal commands and hand signals. Do not trust the dog off-leash unless the area is fenced or blocked in some manner. There is always the chance that a stubborn dog may not come when called. Keep the leash high on his neck and pull him to you very quickly once the command is given. Do not lose your patience, be firm in your commands, and exercise absolute leash control. It is not necessary, however, to be excessively harsh. Stubbornness must not be confused with an inability to learn. A stubborn dog can be taught to respond to this command very well but it takes patience and a superior will.

The sedate dog. This command can be taught outdoors or indoors with one or more trainers. In the early stages of learning the command, do not allow the dog to be taught in an area with distractions. However, it is good for him later on as he progresses. When you give the sedate dog the command to come he will probably walk to you very slowly. Try giving him a lot of praise. If the dog appears somewhat uninvolved, give him a gentle correction and then use a lot of praise. Try to get the dog excited and interested in what's going on. One way to do this is to run backward after you give him the command. By making a game out of it you may get him more involved. Not only will he be forced to come to you but he may also enjoy the session. You may trust dogs of this temperament off-leash for this command. Of course he must still begin with on-leash training.

The aggressive dog. Start training for this command in the house and allow only one trainer and no distractions. This is the type of command that could inspire very aggressive behavior when you pull on the leash for the first time. The dog may try to bite the leash, grab the leash with his paws, or even go after you. Initially work with your voice more than with the leash. Use your voice as much as you can. When you finally have to use the leash for pulling and the dog goes for you, the only thing you can do is suspend him off the ground. This is accomplished by holding the leash high enough so that the dog is lifted up with only his hind legs touching the ground. Keep the collar high on the animal's neck for this possibility. Be more concerned with the dog's coming to you than his sitting once he gets there. Once he starts coming to you, walk backward slowly as you soothe him with verbal praise. Use his name a great deal and tell him that he's a good boy. Do not attempt to use the hand signal for the aggressive dog. That is definitely one way to get bitten. Work on the "Sit" portion of this command after the dog has gotten used to the "Come" part. Once you start teaching him to sit, do not use your hand. Just pull up on the leash and give him the verbal command. It should suffice. It's also much safer.

"Come When Called" is the last command in this basic obedience course. Having gotten this far, you can be proud of yourself and your dog. Congratulations!

15

Mutts of Distinction
(A Photo Gallery)

How MANY TIMES HAS John Garfield shown us the way from poverty to fortune via the boxing ring or the virtuoso violin? In the past we have witnessed John Payne, June Haver, Betty Grable, and Larry Parks rise to public acclaim on the Broadway stage as depicted in film after film. Show business, sports, and artistic endeavors have for many years been a coaxial cable linking one stratum of society to another and allowing its virtuosos to leap from obscurity and class prejudice to recognition and distinction. In recent times ordinary dogs have had more and more opportunity to prove their unique qualities in the fields of entertainment, advertising, and world politics. Some have risen above the restraining leash of class distinction and proven their worth in a truly rags-to-rhinestone tradition.

All but the last three dogs shown in this photo gallery are mutts and mixed-breed dogs belonging to and working for the largest animal talent service on the East Coast, the Dawn Animal Agency of New York City. The last three photos in this gallery show dogs that have become distinctive more for the uniqueness of their ownership and surrounding circumstances than for any display of talent or special abilities. The Dawn Animal Agency has been in existence since 1959 and is uncommonly distinctive from its competition in that it has been firmly rooted in animal humane work since its inception.

Barbara Austin and her sister Bunny have been involved with animals of every description since childhood. When Len Brook, an artist and student of government, married Bunny, the trio pooled their interest in animal rescue work and purchased a farm where they might better care for the animals they saved. This enterprise grew in leaps and bounds to the forty-two acres they now run and its four hundred animals, which include zebras, camels, monkeys, exotic birds, a baby elephant, a llama, and many dozens of dogs and cats, not to mention over seventy horses. Their involvement with animals, from a humane standpoint, rescuing and helping the unwanted, has remained the prime factor in their lives even though the Dawn Animal Agency has grown to its present size and success. Most of the animals that live on the farm have absolutely nothing at all to do with show business or working for a living. It is the talented few that help earn the money necessary to support the majority. This is definitely beyond the tradition of theatrical talent agents.

The owners' involvement in the human movement has brought countless mixed-breed dogs into the Dawn Animal Agency household. L.P., for example, is alive and well at seventeen years of age and was one of Dawn's first stars. Mixed-breed dogs have always been in demand for advertising purposes especially as the "little shaggy dog" type, the "Our Gang" type, or the "Old Yeller" type. These are still standard requests from advertising agencies and Dawn has them all and then some.

One of the best all around performers for Dawn is a mixed-breed named Dutchess. She is really not any one type as she looks different in each and every one of her many TV commercials. Her great asset is her personality. She's quiet and friendly, exuberant but demure. "Dutch" loves kids, which makes her a natural star for children's commercials. She also loves to sleep, which has gotten her many "sleeping at the master's feet" jobs. One other thing about "Dutch": She was adopted from a humane league just a few hours before she was to be destroyed.

Dawn's newest star of the mixed-breed set is Toodles. "Tood" is a Terrier-Poodle cross and was adopted at an animal shelter at the age of six months. Only one and a half years of age, she has proved to be a versatile actress after having appeared in many TV commercials, magazines, and two feature films. So the progression goes on. L.P. is retired, Dutchess is approaching retirement, and Toodles is becoming a star. There have, of course, been numerous other dogs along the way, dogs that have lived their lives and are now gone; dogs that have been retired or are working. The Dawn Animal Agency is an institution that values the mixed-breed, not only as a moneymaker but as a friend and companion. It is important to note that no animal on the Dawn farm is ever mated. Almost every one has been neutered.

When asked where they get their dogs (and other animals) Len Brook answered, "Many dogs, purebred and mixed, end up in a humane shelter or SPCA, most of them being nice dogs. We have gotten ninety percent of our dogs (and other animals) from humane leagues or from people who know us and give us dogs. Some dogs we found on the streets ourselves and kept after advertising for their owners without results. We have one-eared dogs, one-eyed dogs, a dog with three legs, and many others who are simply retired and living out their lives in peace and safety. Those dogs that work are really helping to support the many that do not. At this time we are in the process of forming a nonprofit corporation so that we can solicit for contributions and grants for the purpose of expanding the humane work that we do. We think the nonprofit corporation will be called 'The Sanctuary, Unlimited.' It will be for exotic, equine, and domestic animals.

"There are times when we deal with straight drudgery and become very depressed over a sick or dying animal. There are many heartaches along with the joy. But our business is our life. It demands twenty-four hours out of every day and there's no getting away from it. There is no way to do it if you don't love it."

1. This is *Countess*. It is appropriate to show her first since she was one of the founding members of the Dawn Animal Agency. Like most distinguished canines in this gallery, Countess comes from humble beginnings. She was found wandering the streets of New York city as a stray. With love, understanding, and hours of training she developed into a leading dog model. You may recognize her from one of her numerous credits from ballet, stage, or television. (Dawn Photo)

2. *Gregory* has become a movie star since his successful appearance in the film *Tell Me That You Love Me Junie Moon.* In it he shared the spotlight with Liza Minnelli. Gregory was sent to a local humane society as an untrainable dog. Four weeks after Dawn rescued him he started work on *Junie Moon* as a trained dog. (Dawn Photo)

3. Sultry in her repose is the beautiful *L.P.* She was found abandoned at five days of age. Raised on a baby bottle L.P. went on to become a canine star. She was one of the first dogs to appear for Alpo Dog Food on both the "Today" and "Tonight" shows. A critic said of her appearance in the Broadway play *Before You Go,* "The part could have been written with L.P. in mind." She is seventeen years old and has retired from the business. (Dawn Photo)

4. This is *Toodles* lounging off-camera. She was rescued from a local humane society after having been abandoned. She had star written all over her. In the first six months of 1973 she appeared in two motion pictures, *The Great Gatsby* and *One Across, Two Down*. She has many television commercials to her credit including Sergeant's Dog Products, Tang, and Ralston Purina. (Dawn Photo)

5. Toodles on the set of *The Great Gatsby*.
In it she co-stars with Robert Redford and
Mia Farrow. (Dawn Photo)

6. *Sally.* This is another stray that has been typecast as a "boy's dog" in almost every assignment. She is quite versatile. Not only is she an actress but can do circus work if the assignment calls for it. (Dawn Photo)

7. *Patches.* A Terrier cross is playing "little dog lost" for the umpteenth time. She is one of those canine actresses who can look sad, cute, and lost all at the same time. (Dawn Photo)

8. *Teddy*. For some unknown reason Teddy has not yet made his mark in show business. He keeps trying, though. As a family pet and companion he has no equal. (Dawn Photo)

9. This is *Ginger* at work on a Gainesburgers TV commercial. She is especially sought after because of her warm appeal and well-defined facial expressiveness. (Dawn Photo)

10. & 11. Well known at many advertising agencies, *Betty Lou* is pictured with colleague Bill Murray as they both work on an Alpo Dog Food commercial. Among her other credits is the motion picture *Jeremy*. (Dawn Photo)

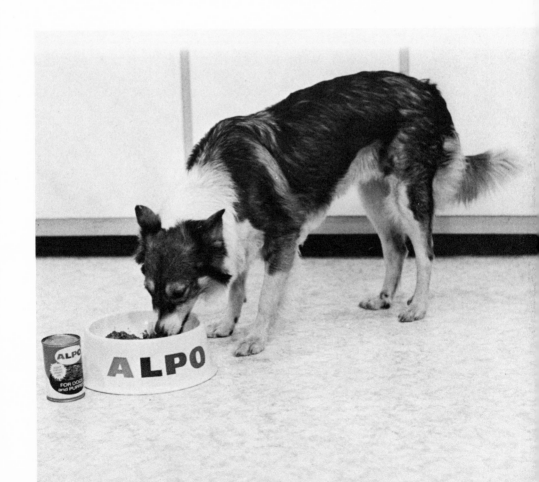

12. Another Dawn star is *Shielia*. Here, she is hard at work on the set posing for a carpet advertisement. (Dawn Photo)

13. This is *Cary*, one of Dawn's retired stars. Known as a student of the Arts she is seen here admiring a statue . (Dawn Photo)

14. & 15. *Ike and Mike.* These are brother and sister twins abandoned on the doorstep of the Dawn farm. Because they are identical they often work together on the same assignment. One backs up the other in the same part. When Ike is tired Mike steps in. The professional competition between the two is intense. (Dawn Photo)

16. *Judy,* part Terrier–part Poodle, all ham. In a rehearsal for the Broadway musical *The Freaking Out of Stephanie Blake,* with Jean Arthur, she played a pirate's dog complete with eye patch. (Dawn Photo)

17. Portrait of a star. Meet *Dutchess,* one of the hardest working and most beloved of the Dawn Repertory. Star quality for a working dog actor means intelligence, warmth, appeal, good temperament, and the ability to adjust to most new situations. Dutchess is the embodiment of all those qualities and more. Her résumé is the envy of all show business. Among her numerous stage appearances she has performed many times in the New York City Opera Company production of *Manon.* On television she has been seen in such commercials as U.S. Savings Bonds, Life Savers, Domino Sugar, Alpo Dog Food (*Dick Cavett Show*), Sunkist Oranges, American Motors, Sanka Coffee, Hartz Mountain Dog Products, and many, many others. She has posed for over 100 still-photograph advertisements, including those for Dr. Pepper, Volkswagen, and the International Ladies Garment Workers Union. She has been called by Norman Griner (Horn-Griner Studio) "Our staff mixed-breed." (Dawn Photo)

18. Spending time with her afternoon companion, Sally the Chimp, Dutchess never talks shop. (Dawn Photo)

19. Dutchess' even temperament indicates that she can move in any circles, especially with her friend Frith, a baby elephant living at the Dawn farm. (Dawn Photo)

21. Taking a stretch, Dutchess displays her
great star quality. (Dawn Photo)

20. June is High Llama at the farm and, obviously,
a very close friend of Dutchess. (Dawn Photo)

23. The furry bundle held by Lieutenant Commander Edward Davis and his wife Elaine is *Mako*, a Vietnamese mongrel home from the war. Davis was a prisoner-of-war for seven and a half years. "When we were shipped to Hanoi in a truck, the guards loaded some dogs in with us," explained Commander Davis. "You might say we were in the same boat. We were prisoners and the dogs were food. When we arrived at our new prison, one by one the dogs would disappear to the kitchen. One day I was raking trash and Mako was helping me. The guard came over and picked her up by the neck and started off toward the kitchen. I ran over with my rake and blocked the guard's path. I stood my ground and pointed at Mako and shouted, "MINE!" From that time on, Mako stayed away from the guards. She always cheered up our harsh existence. Without her, some of us might not have made it. Finally, when the day came, I cut holes in my bag and stuffed her into it, Mako was that important. I rescued Mako," Commander Davis concludes, "but, really, she rescued me."

Mako received the 1973 Animal of the Year Award from the Fund for Animals Incorporated, an international humane organization headed by Cleveland Amory. (United Press International Photo)

22. Taking the spotlight from her illustrious master is *Spaghetti* as she poses with owners Otto Preminger and his son Marc. It was Marc and his sister Victoria who found the lucky dog roaming in New York's Central Park. Returning home with the scruffy mongrel they begged their mother, Hope Preminger, to convince their father that they needed an additional dog in their lives. Mr. Preminger, actor, director, producer, also lives with a Poodle. All are well and living in New York City. Spaghetti has crashed into New York's dog society with grace and style. (Photo by Mark Handler)

24. Royalty! Debarking from the Royal train in King's Cross Station, London, are the Royal pets *Tinker, Pickles,* and *Brush* (left to right). Tinker and Pickles are half Corgi and half Dachshund. Brush is full Corgi. With three of the Royal pets on leads, Her Majesty, The Queen, Elizabeth II, has a smiling handshake for the station manager as he greets her and the Duke of Edinburgh, Prince Philip. One of Queen Elizabeth II's Welsh Corgis whelped a litter of seven puppies sired by Princess Margaret's Dachshund. The breeding was not a misalliance. It was planned by the owners. With pride and satisfaction, underdogs everywhere may take comfort in the knowledge that the Blood Royal has mixed and that somewhere in Buckingham Palace, perhaps under the throne, a wave of canine equality has taken hold. (Photo courtesy of The Press Association, Ltd.)

16

WHERE TO GET A MUTT
(A Directory of Animal Adoption Agencies)

HOORAY FOR THE UNDERDOG

If you're thinking about buying a pet, why not consider a mutt? There are some decided advantages that are very persuasive. One great advantage is the cost. In most cases a donation to a shelter and a neutering fee is all that is involved. If you acquire a dog from a reputable animal shelter, chances are good that the dog will be sound and as healthy as any dog can be.

Did you know that heart malfunctions are three times as common in purebred dogs as in mixed breeds? Did you know that in a scientific study of longevity 59.6 percent of the dogs that lived past seventeen years of age were mutts while only 38.1 percent were purebreds? Many collies tend to have faulty vision. German Shepherds, Boxers, Labradors, and Golden Retrievers suffer more than other dogs from hip dysplasia. Many Scotties suffer from uterine inertia. Look for stomach distension and torsion in Bloodhounds and Irish Setters. Lens luxation is an ailment found largely in Wirehaired Fox Terriers.

The main causes for hereditary abnormalities according to S. F. J. Hodgman and W. B. Singleton, prominent British veterinarians, are the high prices paid for pedigreed dogs, the large number of amateur breeders, the reluctance to cull poor specimens, and a lack of understanding of the principles of breeding. Many physical and psychological abnormalities in dogs are caused by recessive genes that are given the opportunity to surface in one generation of dogs after another by a deliberate process of "unnatural selection." The chances of a mongrel's inheriting genetic abnormalities are smaller than those of a purebred. Although mutts suffer from every illness known to canines, they have a better track record for recovery in many instances than purebreds. These theories have been advanced from the results of many scientifically controlled research programs conducted by international researchers in small-animal medicine.

SUSPENDED SENTENCE

Taking in a dog is a fun thing to do but it can also be an act of humanity and sensitivity. Many millions of dogs and cats are destroyed every year in animal shelters across the country, while millions of others sit in kennels waiting for a family to take them home. This has become a problem of major proportions and relates to the pet-population explosion. According to the Human Society of the United States (HSUS), there would be more dogs and cats than people within ten years if there were no control over the situation. Certainly part of that control is adoption and neutering. There are between 100 and 120 million dogs and cats alive today; about 50 million are homeless. For these reasons representatives of HSUS do not believe that purebred dogs should receive preferential treatment over mongrel dogs. They recommend that American Kennel Club papers be withheld from the person adopting a pet from an animal shelter, even if the papers are available. AKC papers seem to have a mesmerizing effect on some would-be dog owners. They conjure up fantasies of winning dog shows they will never really attend (dog-showing requires much time, money and love of the sport); and stir up get-rich-quick schemes involving the sale of dozens of purebred puppies (a ludicrous myth). The person who demands AKC papers at a shelter is usually going to add to the misery of the unwanted pet population. Many of the most exotic breeds in the world have wound up on the cold steel table of a euthanasia mill.

Adopting a mutt from an animal shelter is very easy and costs very little when compared to the economics of purebred purchasing.

For reasons of humanity and ecology, HSUS has developed a set of procedural standards that it recommends to the hundreds of agencies around the country that offer animals for adoption. These standards are suggested guidelines and therefore vary from shelter to shelter. In summary, they state that no animal should be released for adoption except as a house pet. In order to insure that all adopted animals are cared for properly, they advise local agencies to enter into a legal contract with the new owner, stating that the animal remains the legal property of the adoption agency. In that way the animal may not be sold for profit or given away or harmed by negligence or maltreatment. This type of agreement clearly prevents anyone from profiteering from the sale of animals for laboratory research or any other reason. However, not every agency subscribes to this procedure.

HSUS also suggests that the new owner agree to license the animal, get it vaccinated, provide an identification tag on a collar (an elastic collar for cats), and provide adequate exercise under controlled conditions. But probably the most emphasized point has to do with neutering. HSUS suggests that no unneutered dog or cat be released for adoption unless it is too young to be neutered or is medically incapacitated. It further suggests that if the animal is too young or ill, a fee be paid to the agency to cover the cost of neutering when the animal is old enough or well enough and that the owner return with the animal at the appropriate time. Having the neutering performed by a private veterinarian is optional.

THE DIRECTORY

There are approximately four hundred shelters in the United States operated by nonprofit organizations. Of this total, an estimated seventy-five are city- or county-owned facilities run under municipal contracts.

It is important to understand that animal welfare organizations are individually chartered and autonomous. While these groups use a variety of titles (Humane Society, SPCA, Animal Welfare League, etc.), they are, in fact, all incorporated under similar state laws.

The following listing represents all animal shelters in the United States that are owned or operated by private animal welfare organizations. *They are listed alphabetically by state and then arranged alphabetically by the name of the city or town in which they are located.* Not included in this directory are the estimated twelve to fifteen hundred local-government pounds, shelters, and animal control operations. They too have animals for adoption and can be found in local telephone directories listed under the name of the respective town government.

This directory was compiled by the Humane Society of the United States and was most generously supplied in the hope that many potential dog owners will consider adopting a mongrel or stray dog (or cat), having it neutered, and giving it a good home by adhering to HSUS guidelines for humane treatment. In compiling this information HSUS researched its own office files, sent letters of inquiry to over five hundred organizations, and followed up this effort with phone calls when necessary. The list omits only those organizations whose operations could not be verified through the mail or by telephone. It is important to note that although HSUS has furnished this listing, it has not worked with all of the shelters. Some of them may not strictly conform to HSUS standards. In the case of a shelter that is not properly maintained and where the animals are not properly cared for, please do not misconstrue its inclusion on this list as a blanket approval from HSUS.

On the whole, though, one can safely go to any one of the organizations listed in this directory and find a loving friend, a companion, a terrific dog—an underdog!

ANIMAL SHELTERS IN THE UNITED STATES

Alabama

Calhoun County Humane Society
927 Zinn Drive
Anniston, Alabama 36201
205-237-0528

Athens Humane Society
P. O. Box 725
Athens, Alabama 35611
205-232-7230

The Birmingham Humane Society
27 17th Street, W.
Birmingham, Alabama 35208
205-788-1681

Lauderdale County Humane
Society
P. O. Box 2276
Florence, Alabama 35630
205-764-3492

Montgomery Humane Society
3599 Mobile Highway
Montgomery, Alabama 36108
205-281-0585

Alaska

Alaska SPCA
P. O. Box 776
Anchorage, Alaska 99507
907-279-0578

Arizona

Arizona Humane Society
Sunnyslope Shelter
9235 14th Avenue, N.
Phoenix, Arizona 85021
602-944-2691

Arizona Humane Society
Tri-City Shelter

1211 E. Princess Drive
Tempe, Arizona 85281
602-966-6205

Humane Society of Tucson
3450 N. Kelvin Boulevard
Tucson, Arizona 85716
602-327-6088

Arkansas

Sebastian County Humane Society
3800 Kelley Highway
Fort Smith, Arkansas 72901
501-783-4395

Pet Haven
Route 1
Gassville, Arkansas 72635
501-430-5121

Ozark Humane Society
P. O. Box 542
Harrison, Arkansas 72601
501-365-8752

California

Victor Valley Animal Protective
League
Navajo & Zuni Roads
Apple Valley, California 92307
714-247-2102

North San Diego County Animal
Shelter
2481 Palomar Airport Road
Carlsbad, California 92008
714-729-2312

Rancho-Coastal Humane Society
389 Riqueza Avenue
Encinitas, California 92024
714-753-6413

Escondido Humane Society
163 E. Mission Avenue
Escondido, California 92025
714-745-4362

Central California SPCA
103 S. Hughes Avenue
Fresno, California 93706
209-237-2141

Glendale Humane Society
717 W. Ivy Street
Glendale, California 91204
213-242-1128

Laguna Beach SPCA
20612 Laguna Canyon Road
Laguna Beach, California 92651
714-494-1512

Los Angeles SPCA
West Jefferson Boulevard
Los Angeles, California 90028
213-731-2491

Monterey County SPCA
1002 Monterey-Salinas Highway
Monterey, California 93940
408-373-2631

Humane Society of Marin County
171 Bel Marin Keys Boulevard
Novato, California 94947
415-883-4621

Oakland SPCA of Alameda County
8323 Baldwin Street

Oakland, California 94621
415-569-0702

Oceanside Humane Society
2905 San Luis Rey
Oceanside, California 92054
714-757-4357

Chaffey Community Humane
Society
1010 E. Mission Boulevard
Ontario, California 91762
714-984-2427

Pet Pride
15113 Sunset Boulevard
Pacific Palisades, California 90272
213-459-1703

Desert Humane Society of
Coachella Valley
Indian Avenue
Palm Springs, California 92262
714-329-6741

Humane Society of Palo Alto
Bay Shore Road
Palo Alto, California 94301
415-323-9550

The Pasadena Humane Society
361 S. Raymond Avenue
Pasadena, California 91105
213-792-1016

Humane Society of Pomona Valley
485 Roselawn Avenue
Pomona, California 91766
714-622-1059

Haven Humane Society
7620 Placer Road

Redding, California 96001
916-241-1653

Riverside Humane Society
5791 Fremont Street
Riverside, California 92504
714-688-4340

Sacramento SPCA
2117 Front Street
Sacramento, California
916-449-5623

San Diego Humane Society
887 Sherman Street
San Diego, California 92110
714-297-1813

Pets Unlimited
3170 Sacramento
San Francisco, California 94115
415-931-2580

San Francisco SPCA
2500 Sixteenth Street
San Francisco, California 94103
415-621-1700

Woods Animal Shelter Society
P. O. Box 875
San Luis Obispo, California 93401
805-543-9316

Peninsula Humane Society
1225 Coyote Point Drive
San Mateo, California 94401
415-344-7643

Santa Barbara Humane Society
5399 Overpass Road
Santa Barbara, California 93111
805-964-4777

Humane Society of Santa Clara
Valley
2530 Lafayette Street
Santa Clara, California 95050
408-296-8240

Santa Cruz County Animal Welfare
Association
2200 Seventh Avenue
Santa Cruz, California 95060
408-475-6454

Ventura County Humane Society
788 Mission Rock Road
Santa Paula, California 93060
805-647-4177

Sonoma County Humane Society
5345 Sebastopol Road
Santa Rosa, California 95401
707-542-0882

Colorado

Boulder County Humane Society
2323 55th Street
Boulder, Colorado 80301
303-442-4030

Humane Society of Fremont County
110 S. Rhoades
Canon City, Colorado 81212
303-275-5854

Humane Society of Pikes Peak
Region
633 S. 8th
Colorado Springs, Colorado 80905
303-632-4601

Denver Dumb Friends League
1295 S. Santa Fe Drive

Denver, Colorado 80223
303-778-6135

Mesa County Humane Society
128 Road 30 3/4
Grand Junction, Colorado 81501
303-243-1051

Humane Society of Weld County
P. O. Box 398
Greeley, Colorado 80631
303-356-1299

Colorado Humane Society
Route 1, Box 79
Henderson, Colorado 80640
303-287-9660

Longmont Humane Society
14014 N. 115 Street
Longmont, Colorado
303-772-1232

Connecticut

Pet Animal Welfare Society
P. O. Box 214
Greens Farms, Connecticut 06436
203-227-2175

Connecticut Humane Society
141 Grand Avenue
New Haven, Connecticut
203-777-5468

Connecticut Humane Society
Russell Road
Newington, Connecticut 06111
203-666-3337

Animal Haven, Inc.
89 Mill Road

North Haven, Connecticut 06473
203-239-2641

Connecticut Humane Society
154 Pepper Ridge Road
Stamford, Connecticut 06905
203-324-9269

Connecticut Humane Society
169 Old Colchester Road
Waterford, Connecticut 06385
203-442-8583

Little Guild of St. Francis
West Cornwall, Connecticut 06796
203-672-6178

Connecticut Humane Society
455 E. State Street
Westport, Connecticut 06880
203-227-4137

Delaware

Kent County SPCA
Horsepond Road
Dover, Delaware 19901
302-734-7029

Delaware SPCA
DuPont Highway
South of Georgetown
Georgetown, Delaware 19447
302-856-6361

Delaware SPCA
Route 7
Stanton, Delaware 19804
302-998-2284

Delaware Humane Association
A & Spruce Streets

Wilmington, Delaware 19801
302-655-6710

District of Columbia

Washington Animal Rescue League
71 O Street, N.W.
Washington, D.C. 20001
202-667-5730

Florida

Humane Society of Manatee County
4404 58th Street, W.
Bradenton, Florida 33505
813-756-1946

SPCA of Manatee County
59th Street & 21st Avenue, W.
Bradenton, Florida 33505
813-746-3768

SPCA of Clearwater
S R 590, Route 2
Clearwater, Florida
813-726-4124

West Volusia Humane Society
800 N. Grand Avenue
DeLand, Florida 32720
904-734-2450

Humane Society of Broward County
2070 Griffin Road
Fort Lauderdale, Florida 33312
305-989-3977

Lee County Humane Society
Route 1, Box 560
Fort Myers, Florida 33905
813-334-8640

Humane Society of St. Lucie
County
2720 S. 4th Street
Fort Pierce, Florida 33450
305-461-0687

Humane Society of Fort Walton
Beach
Lovejoy Road
Fort Walton Beach, Florida 32548
904-243-1525

Halifax Humane Society of Volusia
County
W. Eleventh Street at I-95
Holly Hill, Florida 32017
904-255-5364

Jacksonville Humane Society
8464 Beach Boulevard
Jacksonville, Florida 32216
904-725-0780

Southernmost Humane Society
Stock Island
Key West, Florida 33040
305-296-5414

SPCA of St. Petersburg
9099 126th Avenue, N.
Largo, Florida 33540
813-584-8697

Humane Society of Greater Miami
2101 N.W. 95th Street
Miami, Florida 33147
305-696-0800

SPCA of West Pasco
N. Congress Street
New Port Richey, Florida 33552
813-849-1048

Orlando Humane Society
P. O. Box 909
Orlando, Florida 32802
305-843-8130

Humane Society of Pensacola
2480 West Garden Street
Pensacola, Florida 32505
904-432-4250

St. Augustine Humane Society
Route 2, Box 406
St. Augustine, Florida 32084
904-829-2737

Humane Society of Sarasota
2331 15th Street
Sarasota, Florida 33577
813-958-1365

Humane Society of Hillsborough
County
3607 N. Armenia Avenue
Tampa, Florida 33607
813-876-7138; 877-7095

Animal Rescue League of the Palm
Beaches
2401 North Tamarind Avenue
West Palm Beach, Florida 33407
305-833-5692

Humane Society of Vero Beach
1555 Commerce Avenue
Vero Beach, Florida 32960
305-567-2309

Georgia

Atlanta Humane Society
981 Howell Mill Road, N.W.
Atlanta, Georgia 30318
404-875-0771

Augusta Humane Society
6 Milledge
Augusta, Georgia 30904
404-736-0186

Humane Society of Glynn County
Route 2, Box 39E
Brunswick, Georgia 31520
912-264-1191

Humane Society of Chatham-
Savannah
7215 Mederiar Road
Savannah, Georgia 31404
912-354-9515

Hawaii

Hawaiian Humane Society
2700 Waialae Avenue
Honolulu, Hawaii 96814
808-946-2187

Idaho

Idaho Humane Society
Gowen Field Road, Route 3
Boise, Idaho 83705
208-343-3451

Twin Falls County Humane Society
P. O. Box 986
Twin Falls, Idaho 83301
208-734-2493

Illinois

Belleville Area Humane Society
1301 S. 11th Street Road

Belleville, Illinois 62221
618-233-9062

Champaign County Humane
Society
West Springfield Avenue Road
Bondville, Illinois 61815
217-863-2230

Anti-Cruelty Society
157 W. Grand Avenue
Chicago, Illinois 60610
312-644-8338

Illinois Citizens Animal Welfare
League
6224 S. Wabash Avenue
Chicago, Illinois 60637
312-667-0088

Humane Society of Danville
1225 N. Collett Street
Danville, Illinois 61832
217-446-4110

Alton Area Animal Aid Association
East Delmar Road, Route #5
Godfrey, Illinois 62035
618-462-3721

Jackson County Humane Society
Route #2
Murphysboro, Illinois 62966
618-457-2362

Tazewell Animal Shelter
River Road
Pekin, Illinois 61554
309-346-1838

Quincy Humane Society
1019 S. Front Street

Quincy, Illinois 62301
217-223-8786

Animal Welfare League
5401 Beltlinerd
Rockford, Illinois
815-962-4051

Humane Society of North Central
Illinois
LaFox
South Elgin, Illinois 60177
312-697-2880

Indiana

The Greater Bloomington
and Monroe County Humane
Association
3410 South Highway 37
Bloomington, Indiana 47401
812-339-4248

Clay County Humane Society
R.R. 4
Brazil, Indiana 47834
812-446-5126

Animal Welfare League
of Montgomery County
North Washington
Crawfordsville, Indiana 47933
317-362-8846

Elkhart County Humane Society
County Road 19
Elkhart, Indiana 46514
219-848-4225

Fort Wayne Humane Society
2225 Dwenger Avenue

Fort Wayne, Indiana 46803
219-423-7151; 743-4962

Gary Humane Society
6800 E. 7th Avenue
Gary, Indiana 46403
219-938-3339

Humane Society—Calumet Area
6546 Columbia Avenue
Hammond, Indiana 46320
219-931-2507

Humane Society of Hobart
State Road 30
Hobart, Indiana 46342
219-942-8506

Indianapolis Humane Society
7929 N. Michigan Road
Indianapolis, Indiana 46268
317-293-5650

Kokomo Humane Society
713 N. Elizabeth Street
Kokomo, Indiana 46901
317-452-6224

Tippecanoe County Humane
Association
P. O. Box 134
Lafayette, Indiana 47902
317-474-5222

Marion-Grant County Humane
Society
2768 E. Tulip Drive
Marion, Indiana 46952
317-674-7440

Humane Society of St. Joseph
County

2506 Liberty Drive
Mishawaka, Indiana 46544
219-255-4726

Home for Friendless Animals
R.R. 4, Box 195
Noblesville, Indiana 46060
317-773-2460

Terre Haute Humane Society
1811 S. Fruitridge Avenue
Terre Haute, Indiana 47803
812-232-0293

Lakeland Humane Association
800 East Winona Avenue
Warsaw, Indiana 46580
219-267-3008

Iowa

Humane Society of Linn County
R.R. 3, Mt. Vernon Road, S.E.
Cedar Rapids, Iowa 52401
319-362-6288

Humane Society of Scott County
2134 W. River Drive
Davenport, Iowa 52802
319-326-2591

Animal Rescue League of Iowa
5452 N.E. 22nd
Des Moines, Iowa 50313
515-262-9503

Dubuque Humane Society
3398 Center Grove Drive
Dubuque, Iowa 52001
319-582-6766

Animal Rescue League of Marshalltown

Marshalltown, Iowa 50158
515-753-9046

Humane Society of Cerro Gordo
County
R.R. 4
Mason City, Iowa 50401
515-423-6366

Sioux City Humane Society
1665 18th Street
Sioux City, Iowa 51103
712-252-2614

Waterloo Humane Society
Airline Highway
Waterloo, Iowa 50701
319-232-6887

Kansas

The Humane Society
of Wyandotte County
316 Minnesota Avunue
Kansas City, Kansas 66101
913-371-3869

Franklin County Humane Society
R.R. 1
Ottawa, Kansas 66067
913-242-2967

Helping Hands Humane Society
2625 Rochester Road
Topeka, Kansas 66617
913-233-7325

Kansas Humane Society
4218 Southeast Boulevard
Wichita, Kansas 67210
316-683-6596

Kentucky

Bowling Green–Warren County
Humane Society
902 W. Main Street
Bowling Green, Kentucky 42101
502-842-8572

SPCA of Kenton County
3-L Highway
Fort Mitchell, Kentucky 41017
606-331-2374

Franklin County Humane Society
Clinton Street
Frankfort, Kentucky 40601
502-223-7914

Humane Society of Henderson
County
Drury Lane
Henderson, Kentucky 42420
502-826-8966

Lexington Humane Society
775 Chinoe Road Extended
Lexington, Kentucky 40502
606-252-4931

Kentucky Humane Society—Animal
Rescue League
241 Steedly Drive
Louisville, Kentucky 40214
502-366-3355

Hopkins County Humane Society
P. O. Box 96
Madisonville, Kentucky 42431
502-821-8965; 821-6855

McCracken County Humane
Society

N. Sixth Street
Paducah, Kentucky 42001
502-443-5923; 443-7363

Louisiana

St. Tammany Parish Humane
Society
Harrison Road
Covington, Louisiana 70433
504-892-0551

Caddo Shreveport Humane Society
823 Fairview
Shreveport, Louisiana 71104
318-868-7974

Slidell Humane Society
Terrace Avenue
Slidell, Louisiana 70458
504-643-8866

Animal Havens League
Antonine & Tchoupitoulas Streets
New Orleans, Louisiana 70115
No phone listed

Louisiana SPCA
1319 Japonica Street
New Orleans, Louisiana 70117
504-944-7446

Maine

Lewiston-Auburn SPCA
Old Poland Road
Auburn, Maine 04210
207-783-2311

Kennebec Valley Humane Society

Pet Haven Lane
Augusta, Maine 04330
207-623-8765

The Bangor Humane Society
693 Mt. Hope Avenue
Bangor, Maine 04401
207-942-8902

Boothbay Harbor Humane Society
Boothbay Harbor, Maine 04538
207-633-4457

Brunswick Humane Society
Golf Link Road
Brunswick, Maine 04011
207-725-5051

Down East Animal Welfare
Woods Street
Southwest Harbor, Maine 04679
207-244-3178

Animal Welfare Society
Holland Road
West Kennebunk, Maine 04094
207-985-3244

Maryland

SPCA of Anne Arundel County
1815 Bay Ridge Avenue
Annapolis, Maryland 21403
301-268-4388

Maryland SPCA
3300 Falls Road
Baltimore, Maryland 21211
301-235-8826

Cecil County SPCA

R.D. 1
Chesapeake City, Maryland 21915
301-885-5050

Humane Society of Kent County
P.O. Box 31
Chestertown, Maryland 21620
301-778-3648; 778-1548

Talbot County Humane Society
Easton, Maryland 21601
301-822-0107

Animal Welfare Society of Howard
County
Waterloo & Davis Roads
Ellicott City, Maryland 21043
301-465-4350

Humane Society of Harford County
2208 Connolly Road
Fallston, Maryland 21047
301-877-9744

Frederick County Humane Society
Gas House Pike
Frederick, Maryland 21701
301-663-3981

SPCA of Washington County
Marshall Street Ext.
Hagerstown, Maryland 21740
301-733-2060

Humane   Society   of   Baltimore
County
Nicodemus Road
Reistertown, Maryland 21136
301-833-3300

Wicomico Humane Society
Marine Road

Salisbury, Maryland 21801
301-749-2003

Montgomery County Humane
Society
9710 Brookville Road
Silver Spring, Maryland 20910
301-585-2933

Humane Society of Carroll County
Westminster, Maryland 21157
301-848-4810

Massachusetts

Animal Rescue League of Boston
Tremont & Arlington Streets
Boston, Massachusetts 02117
617-426-9170

Massachusetts SPCA
180 Longwood Avenue
Boston, Massachusetts 02115
617-731-2000

Massachusetts SPCA
226 Pearl Street
Brockton, Massachusetts 02401
617-586-2053

Massachusetts SPCA
Martha's Vineyard
Edgartown, Massachusetts 02539
617-627-8662

Greenfield Area Animal Shelter
French King Highway
Greenfield, Massachusetts 01301
413-773-3148

Massachusetts SPCA

State Road, Route 28
Hyannis, Massachusetts 02601
617-775-0940 (Centerville)

Lowell Humane Society
951 Broadway Street
Lowell, Massachusetts 01854
617-452-7781

Massachusetts SPCA
400 Broadway
Methuen, Massachusetts 01844
617-687-7453

Massachusetts SPCA
Crooked Lane
Nantucket, Massachusetts 02554
617-228-1491

Animal Rescue League of New
Bedford
38 Hillman Street
New Bedford, Massachusetts 02740
617-992-4203

The Buddy Dog Humane Society
56 Dakin Road
North Sudbury,
Massachusetts 01776
617-443-8626

Pepperell Humane Society
41 Cranberry Street
Pepperell, Massachusetts 01463
617-433-2687

Massachusetts SPCA
108 Cadwell Road
Pittsfield, Massachusetts 01201

Massachusetts SPCA
53057 Bliss Street

Springfield, Massachusetts 01105
413-785-1221

Massachusetts SPCA
Cherry Street
Wenham, Massachusetts 01984
617-468-2466

Michigan

Lenawee County Humane Society
Academy Road
Adrian, Michigan 49221
313-263-1432

Humane Society of Washtenaw
County
3100 Cherry Hill Road
Ann Arbor, Michigan 48105
313-662-5585

Calhoun County Humane Society
64 S. Edison
Battle Creek, Michigan 49017
616-963-1796

Humane Society of Berrien County
Britain & Crystal Avenues
Benton Harbor, Michigan 49022
616-927-3303

Anti-Cruelty Association
13569 Joseph Campau Avenue
Detroit, Michigan 48212
313-891-7188

Michigan Humane Society
Chrysler Expressway
Detroit, Michigan
313-872-3400

Kent County Humane Society
1980 Bristol Avenue, N.W.
Grand Rapids, Michigan 49504
616-453-7757

Dickinson County Humane Society
P.O. Box 237
Iron Mountain, Michigan 49801
906-774-1005

Kalamazoo Humane Society
3915 Stadium Drive
Kalamazoo, Michigan 49001
616-375-5480

Ingham County Humane Society
1713 Sunset Avenue
Lansing, Michigan 48917
517-371-1492

Isabella County Humane Society
S. Isabella Road
Mount Pleasant, Michigan 48858
517-773-9721; 773-9871

Emmet County Humane Society
Route 4, East Bay View Drive
Petoskey, Michigan 49771
616-347-2396

Michigan Animal Rescue League
790 Featherstone Road
Pontiac, Michigan 48058
313-335-9290

Al-Van Humane Society
Dunbley Avenue
South Haven, Michigan 49090
616-637-5062

Cherryland Humane Society
Barlow & Keystone Roads

Traverse City, Michigan 49684
616-946-5116

Macomb County Humane Society
11350 22 Mile Road
Utica, Michigan 48087
313-731-9210

Michigan Humane Society
37255 Marquette
Westland, Michigan 48185
313-721-7300

Minnesota

Animal Humane Society
845 France Avenue N.
Minneapolis, Minnesota 55422
612-522-4325

Humane Society of Northern
Minnesota
Nordquist Animal Shelter
S. Forest Avenue
Park Rapids, Minnesota 56470
218-732-3165

St. Paul Humane Society
Beulah Lane
St. Paul, Minnesota 55108
612-646-2184

Mississippi

Harrison County Humane Society
6500 Washington Avenue
Gulfport, Mississippi 39501
601-863-3354

The Mississippi Animal Rescue
League

P.O. Box 11264
Delta Station
Jackson, Mississippi 39213

Missouri

Animal Protective Association
1705 S. Hanley Road
Brentwood, Missouri 63144
314-645-4610

Central Missouri Humane Society
1306 Creary Spring Road
Columbia, Missouri 65201
314-443-3893

Joplin Humane Society
Route 3
Joplin, Missouri 64801
417-623-3642

Wayside Waifs
3901 E. 119th Street
Kansas City, Missouri 64137
816-763-8151

Humane Society of Missouri
1210 Macklind Avenue
St. Louis, Missouri 63110
314-647-8800

Greene County Humane Society
Route 6
Springfield, Missouri 63103
417-833-2526

Montana

Missoula County Humane Society
Route 2, Mullen Road

Missoula, Montana 59801
406-549-3939

Nebraska

Central Nebraska Humane Society
1324 Stuhr Road
Grand Island, Nebraska
308-384-9133

Humane Society
2320 Park Boulevard
Lincoln, Nebraska 68502
402-477-3949

Nebraska Humane Society
8801 Fort Streét
Omaha, Nebraska 63134
402-571-0702

Nevada

Nevada Humane Society
2200 Mill Street
Reno, Nevada 89504
702-329-4228

New Hampshire

New Hampshire Humane Society
P.O. Box 572
Laconia, New Hampshire
603-524-2610

Monadnock Region Humane
Society
Route 10
West Swanzey, New Hampshire
03469
603-352-9011

New Jersey

Humane Society of Atlantic County
1801 Absecon Boulevard
Atlantic City, New Jersey 08401
609-344-0346

The Shelter
185 Brick Boulevard
Brick Town, New Jersey 08723
201-477-2446

Cape May County SPCA
Box 570, R.D. 2
Cape May, New Jersey 08204
609-884-4285

St. Hubert's Giralda
575 Woodland Avenue
Chatham Township, New Jersey
07940
201-377-8877

Animal Welfare Association of
Camden County
P.O. Box 35
Collingswood, New Jersey
609-424-2588

Monmouth County SPCA
R.D. 1, Box 260, Wall Street
Eatontown, New Jersey 07724
201-542-0040

Montclair Animal Welfare League
194 State Highway 10
Hanover, New Jersey 07936
201-227-3281

Hudson County SPCA
484 Johnston Avenue
Jersey City, New Jersey 07302
201-435-3557

Lakeland Animal Haven
29 Pine Street
Kenvil, New Jersey 07847
201-584-1415

Camden County SPCA
Old Berlin & Shadyside Avenues
Lindenwold, New Jersey 08021
609-931-8009

Burlington County SPCA
P.O. Box 164
Mount Holly, New Jersey 08060
609-267-7283

New Jersey SPCA-Middlesex
29 Somerset Street
New Brunswick, New Jersey 08901
201-247-1825

Associated Humane Societies
124 Evergreen Avenue
Newark, New Jersey 07114
201-243-5060

Passaic County Animal Welfare
Society
25 Church Street
Paterson, New Jersey 07505
201-525-8925

Plainfield Humane Society
75 Rock Avenue
Plainfield, New Jersey 07060
201-754-0300

Union County SPCA
90 St. Georges Avenue
Rahway, New Jersey 07065
201-382-6100

Somerset County Humane Society

P.O. Box 551
Somerville, New Jersey 08876
201-526-3330

Ocean County SPCA
Box 344
Toms River, New Jersey 08753
609-693-2931

Cumberland County SPCA
1376 W. Sherman Avenue
Vineland, New Jersey 08360
609-691-1500

New Mexico

Animal Humane Association of New
Mexico
615 Virginia Street, S.E.
Albuquerque, New Mexico 87108
505-255-5523

Humane Society of Lincoln County
P.O. Box 722
Ruidoso, New Mexico 88345
505-378-4125

Roswell Humane Society
312 E. Walnut Street
Roswell, New Mexico 88201
505-623-6500

Santa Fe Animal Shelter
1920 Cerrillos Road
Santa Fe, New Mexico 87501
505-983-7471

New York

Mohawk and Hudson River

Humane Society
7 Elk Street
Albany, New York 12207
518-465-5251

Amsterdam SPCA
Route 5-S
Amsterdam, New York 12010
518-842-8050

Cayuga County SPCA
York Street
Auburn, New York 13021
315-253-5841

Bath Area Humane Society
P.O. Box 308, R.D. 2
Hammondsport Road
Bath, New York 14810
607-776-3039

Broome County Humane Society
2 Jackson Street
Binghamton, New York 13904
607-724-3709

Westchester County SPCA
North State Road
Briarcliff Manor, New York 10510
914-941-2894

ASPCA Bronx Shelter
420 Morris Park Avenue
Bronx, New York 10460
212-892-8500

ASPCA Brooklyn Shelter
233 Butler Street
Brooklyn, New York 11217
212-875-9580

Putnam County Humane Society

Carmel, New York 10512
914-225-7777

Ada Howe Kent Memorial Shelter
River Road
Calverton, New York 11933
516-727-5731

Corning–Painted Post Area
Humane Society
Route 414
Corning, New York 14830
607-962-2124

Cortland County SPCA
161 McLean Road
Cortland, New York 13045
607-753-3780

The Humane Society of Central
Delaware County
P.O. Box 483
East Delhi, New York 13753

Elmira SPCA
P.O. Box 3001, Westside Station
Elmira, New York 14905
607-732-1827

ASPCA Western Westchester
Shelter
Old Saw Mill River Road
Elmsford, New York 10523
914-592-7334

Humane Society of Rochester &
Monroe County
99 Victor Road
Fairport, New York 14450
716-232-1330

Chautauqua County Humane
Society

E. Elmwood Avenue
Falconer, New York 14733
716-487-6882

Humane Association Shelter
Route 5
Fayetteville, New York 13066

Animal Haven
190-30 99th Avenue
Flushing, New York 11369

Washington County SPCA
East River Road
Fort Edward, New York 12828
518-747-3452

Herkimer County Humane Society
Route 5-S
Fort Herkimer, New York 13407
315-866-3255

Long Island Humane and Dog Protective Association
2 Rider Place
Freeport, New York 11520
516-278-4340

ASPCA Glen Cove Shelter
Pratt Boulevard Ext.
Glen Cove, New York 11542
516-676-5913

Ulster County SPCA
c/o Glenford, New York 12433

Schenectady Animal Shelter
Alplaus Road
Glenville, New York 12302
518-374-3944

Humane Society of Fulton County

P.O. Box 688
Gloversville, New York 12078

Westchester Shore Humane Society
7 Harrison Avenue
Harrison, New York 10528
914-835-3332

Humane Society Animal Shelter
Bald Hill
Hornell, New York 14843
607-324-1270

Columbia-Greene Humane Society
Box 424
N. Claverack, Route 66
Hudson, New York 12534
518-828-6044

Dutchess County SPCA
Violet Avenue
Hyde Park, New York 12601
914-452-1640

Tompkins County SPCA
Hanshaw Road, Route 2
Ithaca, New York 14850
607-257-1822

ASPCA Queens Shelter
94-27 158th Street
Jamaica, New York 11433
212-739-4041

ASPCA Long Beach Shelter
70 Water Street
Long Beach, New York 11561
516-431-0660

Lewis County Humane Society
Court House
Lowville, New York 11637

Humane Society of Middletown
R.D. 4
Middletown, New York 10940
914-342-2243

Nesconset Smithtown Animal
Shelter
Nesconset, New York 11767

SPCA
Route 207, P.O. Box 125
Newburgh, New York 12550
914-564-6810

Hi-Tor Animal Shelter
c/o 416 S. Mountain Road
New City, New York 10956

ASPCA Manhattan Shelter
441 E. 92nd Street
New York, New York 10028
212-876-7700

Bide-a-Wee Home Association
Manhattan Shelter
410 E. 38th Street
New York, New York 10016
212-532-4455

Humane Society of New York
313 E. 58th Street
New York, New York 10022
212-752-4840

New Rochelle Humane Society
Emmett Terrace
New Rochelle, New York 10805
914-632-2925

Newburgh SPCA
Route 207
Newburgh, New York 12550
914-564-6810

Niagara County SPCA
Military Road
Niagara Falls, New York
716-297-2490

Chenango County SPCA
Wells Road
Norwich, New York 13815

Rockland County SPCA
Box 24
Nyack, New York 10960

Cataraugus County SPCA
Route 16
Hinsdale Road
Olean, New York 14760

Humane Society of Port Jervis–
Deerpark
R.D. 2
Port Jervis, New York 12771
914-856-3677

North Shore Animal League
22 South Street
Port Washington, New York 11050
516-883-7575

Dutchess County SPCA
476 Violet Avenue
Poughkeepsie, New York 12601
914-452-1640

Sullivan County SPCA
Route 17
Rock Hill, New York 12775
914-796-3120

Rome Humane Society
Lamphear Box 428
Rome, New York 13440
315-337-6260

ASPCA Richmond Shelter
4 Willow Avenue
Rosebank, New York 10305
212-447-0122

Hampton Animal Shelter
Brick Kiln Road
Sag Harbor, New York 11963
516-725-9730

Animal Welfare League of Saratoga
County
95 Oak Street
Saratoga, New York 12866

Sho-Field Kennels
Ballston Spa
Saratoga, New York 12866

Central Westchester Humane
Society
Box 187
Scarsdale, New York 10583

Delaware Valley Humane Society
Sidney, New York 13838
607-369-9238

Oyster Bay Animal Shelter
Miller Place
Syosset, New York 11791

SPCA of Central New York
5878 E. Molloy Road
Syracuse, New York 13211
315-454-4479

Adirondack Animal Humane Association
Ticonderoga, New York 12883
518-585-3352

Erie County SPCA

205 Ensminger Road
Tonawanda, New York 14150

Stevens-Swan Humane Society of
Oneida County
172 N. Genessee Street
Utica, New York 13503
315-733-7830

Humane Society of Walden
23 Rifton Place
Walden, New York 12586
914-778-1627

Bide-a-Wee Home Association
Wantagh Shelter
Wantagh & Beltagh Avenues
Wantagh, New York 11793
516-785-4079

Orange County Suburban Humane
Society
P.O. Box 61
Kings Highway
Warwick, New York 10990
914-986-2473

Bide-a-Wee Home Association
P. G. Wodehouse Animal Shelter
Old Country Road
West Hampton, New York 11977
516-325-0200

North Country SPCA
North Shore Road
Westport, New York 12993
518-962-8604

North Carolina

North Carolina SPCA

20 Utopia Road
Asheville, North Carolina 28805
704-253-8862

Wake County SPCA
Route 2, Box 71
Garner, North Carolina 27529
919-772-3723

North Dakota

(no societies listed in HSUS files)

Ohio

Ashtabula County Animal Protective League
3426 Blake Road
Ashtabula, Ohio 44004
215-997-5620

Athens County Humane Society
Box 765
Athens, Ohio 45701
614-593-6864

Stark County Humane Society
1715 Ninth Street, N.E.
Canton, Ohio 44705
216-453-5529

Ross County Humane Society
Lick Run Road, Route 4
Chillicothe, Ohio 45601
614-775-6808

Hamilton County SPCA
3949 Colerain Avenue
Cincinnati, Ohio 45223
513-541-6100

Humane Society of Columbus
2770 Groveport Road
Columbus, Ohio 43215
614-224-7800

Montgomery County Humane Society
451 W. Third Street
Dayton, Ohio 45402
513-225-4302

Lorain County Animal Protective League
2171 West River Road, S.
Elyria, Ohio 44035
216-323-4321

The Humane Association of Miami Valley
5225 Hamilton-Trenton Road
Hamilton, Ohio 45011
513-867-5727

Lima Allen County Humane Society
1125 Sereff Road
Lima, Ohio 45805
419-991-5720

Mansfield Humane Society
395 Lantz Road
Mansfield, Ohio 44906

Washington County Humane Society
Dodds Run, Box 5
Marietta, Ohio 45750
614-373-5959

Marion County Humane Society
Mt. Vernon Road
Prospect, Ohio 43342
614-494-2344

Portage County Animal Protective League
903 E. Lake Street
Ravenna, Ohio 44266
216-296-4022

Seneca County Humane Society
925 N. Water Street
Tiffin, Ohio 44883
419-447-5704

Toledo Humane Society
410 S. Erie Street
Toledo, Ohio 43601
419-242-9571

Oklahoma

Washington County SPCA
Old Dewey Highway
Bartlesville, Oklahoma 74003
918-336-1557

Oregon

Benton Humane Society
526 S.W. Third
Corvallis, Oregon 97330
503-752-5031

Lane Humane Society
350 N. Greenhill Road
Eugene, Oregon 97402
503-689-1503

Southern Oregon Humane Society
2901 Table Rock Road
Medford, Oregon 97501
503-779-3201

Oregon Humane Society
1067 N.E. Columbia Boulevard
Portland, Oregon 97211
503-285-0641

Humane Society of the Willamette Valley
4246 Turner Road, S.E.
Salem, Oregon 97302
503-585-5900

Pennsylvania

Lehigh County Humane Society
640 Dixon Street
Allentown, Pennsylvania 18103
215-797-1205

Central Pennsylvania Humane Society
1837 E. Pleasant Valley Boulevard
Altoona, Pennsylvania 16602
814-942-4931

Pennsylvania SPCA
Danville Highway
Bloomsburg, Pennsylvania 17815
717-275-0340

McKean County SPCA
R.D. 1
Bradford, Pennsylvania 16701
814-362-8850; 362-1642

Butler County Humane Society
Herman Road, R.D. 3
Butler, Pennsylvania 16001
412-287-0800

Pennsylvania SPCA
R.D. 1

Centre Hall, Pennsylvania 16828
814-364-1725

Montgomery County SPCA
19 E. Ridge Pike
Conshohocken, Pennsylvania 19428
215-825-0111

Pennsylvania SPCA
R.D. 4
Danville, Pennsylvania 17821
717-275-0340

Monroe County SPCA
Wild Animal Farm Road
East Stroudsburg, Pennsylvania 18301
717-421-6761

Washington County Humane Society
P.O. Box 66
Eighty-Four, Pennsylvania 15330
412-222-2615

Northwestern Pennsylvania Humane Society
Erie, Pennsylvania
814-866-7411

Animal Rescue League of Berks County
P.O. Box 293
Geigertown, Pennsylvania 19523
215-373-8830

Humane Society of Harrisburg
7790 Grayson Road
Harrisburg, Pennsylvania 17111
717-564-3320

Cambria County SPCA

St. Clair Road
Johnstown, Pennsylvania 15905
814-255-2086

Bucks County SPCA
794 Street Road
Lahaska, Pennsylvania 18931
215-794-7425

Humane League of Lancaster County
2195 Lincoln Highway E.
Lancaster, Pennsylvania 17602
717-393-6551

Delaware County SPCA
555 Sandy Bank Road
Media, Pennsylvania 19063
215-606-1370

Schuylkill County SPCA
Hillside Road
Minersville, Pennsylvania 17954
717-622-7769

Beaver County Humane Society
Beaver Valley Mall
Monaca, Pennsylvania 15061
412-775-5801

Susquehanna County Humane Society
100 Grow Avenue
Montrose, Pennsylvania 18801
717-278-1228

Lawrence County Humane Society
Pearson Mill Road
New Castle, Pennsylvania 16101
412-654-8520

Morris Animal Refuge

1242 Lombard Street
Philadelphia, Pennsylvania 19147
215-735-3256

Pennsylvania SPCA
350 Erie Avenue
Philadelphia, Pennsylvania 19134
215-426-6300

Women's SPCA
30th & Clearfield Streets
Philadelphia, Pennsylvania 19132
215-225-4500

Animal Friends
2643 Penn Avenue
Pittsburgh, Pennsylvania 15222
412-566-7533

Animal Rescue League of Pittsburgh
6620 Hamilton Avenue
Pittsburgh, Pennsylvania 15206
412-661-6452

Western Pennsylvania Humane Society
1101 Western Avenue
Pittsburgh, Pennsylvania 15233
412-321-4625

Humane Society of Berks County
1801 N. 11th Street
Reading, Pennsylvania 19604
215-921-2348

Humane Society of Lackawanna County
1900 E. Gidson Street
Scranton, Pennsylvania 18510
717-343-8722

Pennsylvania SPCA
R.D. 1
Stroudsburg, Pennsylvania 18360
717-421-6761

York County SPCA
R.D. 1
Thomasville, Pennsylvania 17364
717-792-1810

Animal Rescue League of Pittsburgh
Rosedale Kennels
Verona Road
Verona, Pennsylvania 15147
412-793-1135

Pennsylvania SPCA
R.D. 3
Wellsboro, Pennsylvania 16901
717-724-3687

Chester County SPCA
1212 Phoenixville Pike
West Chester, Pennsylvania 19380
215-692-6113

The SPCA of Luzerne County
524 E. Main Street, Fox Hill
Wilkes-Barre, Pennsylvania 18702
717-825-4111

Lycoming County SPCA
2805 Reach Road
Williamsport, Pennsylvania 17701
717-322-4646

Rhode Island

Robert Potter League for Animals
15 Harrington Street
Newport, Rhode Island 02840
401-846-8276

Providence Animal Rescue League
34 Elbow Street
Providence, Rhode Island 02903
401-421-1399

South Carolina

John Ancrum SPCA
Dupont Road
Charleston, South Carolina 29409
803-766-0936

Richland SPCA
Calhoun Street
Columbia, South Carolina
803-256-7367

South Dakota

Sioux Falls Humane Society
2105 North Drive
Sioux Falls, South Dakota 57104
605-338-4441

Tennessee

Chattanooga Humane Educational
Society
212 N. Highland Park Avenue
Chattanooga, Tennessee 37404
615-622-8913

Knox County Humane Society
Millwood Road, S.W.
Knoxville, Tennessee 37918
615-577-2218

The Memphis Humane Society
Tchulahoma Road
Memphis, Tennessee 38118
901-362-5310

Morristown-Hamblen Humane
Society
Morris Boulevard & Dice Street
Morristown, Tennessee 37814
615-581-1494

Nashville Humane Association
108 Harding Place
Nashville, Tennessee 37205
615-352-4030

Texas

Humane Society of Austin & Travis
County
1156 West First Street
Austin, Texas 78703
512-478-9325

Dallas SPCA
P.O. Box 803
Dallas, Texas 75221
214-376-8113

SPCA of Galveston County
Route 1, Box 154M
Dickenson, Texas 77539
713-559-2626

El Paso County Humane Society
325 Shelter Place
El Paso, Texas 79905
915-532-6971

Houston SPCA
519 Studemont Street
Houston, Texas 77007
713-861-1023

Houston Humane Society
14700 Almeda Road

Houston, Texas 77045
713-433-6421

Humane Society of Wichita County
Iowa Park Road
Iowa Park, Texas 76367
817-592-4542

Cherokee County Humane Society
800 Woodlawn
Jacksonville, Texas 75766
214-586-9723

Humane Society of Angelina
County
Ellen Trout Park
Lufkin, Texas 75901
713-632-7550

Humane Society of Bexar County
307 W. Jones
San Antonio, Texas 78215
512-226-7461

Humane Society of Smith County
Box 3151
Tyler, Texas 75701
214-597-2471

Six Flags Humane Society
400 Victoria Bank & Trust Building
Victoria, Texas 77901
512-573-7414

Utah

The Humane Society of Utah
4613 S. 4000, W.
Salt Lake City, Utah 84119
801-298-3548

Vermont

Burlington Humane Society
633 S. Queens City Park Road
Burlington, Vermont 05401
802-862-0135

Central Vermont Humane Society
Box 687
Montpelier, Vermont 05602
802-223-5674

Rutland County Humane Society
Stevens Road
Pittsford, Vermont 05763
802-483-6700

Springfield Humane Society
Springfield, Vermont 05156
802-885-3997

Virginia

Alexandria Animal Welfare League
910 S. Payne Street
Alexandria, Virginia 22314
703-750-6597

Animal Welfare League of Arlington
2800 S. Taylor Street
Arlington, Virginia 22206
703-931-9241

Albemarle SPCA
Box 1883
Charlottesville, Virginia 22903
703-973-5959

Culpeper Animal Welfare League
Orange Road

Culpeper, Virginia 22701
703-825-9599; 825-9002; 825-1581

Fredericksburg SPCA
1523 William Street
Fredericksburg, Virginia 22401
703-373-9008

Humane Society of Warren County
Route 618
Front Royal, Virginia 22630
703-635-4734

Peninsula SPCA
213 Salters Creek Road
Hampton, Virginia 23361
703-722-1926

Rockbridge SPCA
Box 528
Lexington, Virginia 24450
703-463-5123

Lynchburg Humane Society
3305 Naval Reserve Street
Lynchburg, Virginia 24501
703-846-1438

Norfolk SPCA
916 Ballentine Boulevard
Norfolk, Virginia 23504
703-622-3319

SPCA-Eastern Shore, Inc.
Route 13
Onley, Virginia 23410
703-787-9732

Portsmouth Humane Society
2720 Frederick Boulevard
Portsmouth, Virginia
703-397-6004

Richmond SPCA
1600 Chamberlayne Avenue
Richmond, Virginia 23222
703-643-6785

Roanoke Valley SPCA
1313 Eastern Avenue, N.E.
Roanoke, Virginia 24012
703-344-4840

Virginia Beach SPCA
1098 Farm Road
Virginia Beach, Virginia 23458
703-428-3601

Fauquier SPCA
Springs Road
Warrenton, Virginia 22186
703-347-7148; 347-2901

Williamsburg Area SPCA
Route 143
Williamsburg, Virginia 23185
703-229-3027

Washington

Whatcom County Humane Society
3825 Williamson Way
Bellingham, Washington 98225
206-733-2080

Kitsap County Humane Society
Charleston Beach Road
Bremerton, Washington 98310
206-377-7043

The Animals' Crusaders
2015 Hoyt Avenue
Everett, Washington 98201
206-259-1820

Thurston County Humane Society
320 Thurston Avenue, E.
Olympia, Washington 98501
206-943-3640

Spokane Humane Society
W704 Broadway
Spokane, Washington 99201
509-328-8920

Tacoma-Pierce County Humane
Society
2608 Center Street
Tacoma, Washington 98409
206-383-2733

Humane Society of Vancouver-
Clark County
2323 N.W. 26th Ext.
Vancouver, Washington 98660
206-693-4746

Yakima County Humane Society
1903 S. First Street
Yakima, Washington 98901
509-457-6854

West Virginia

Charleston Humane Association
1248 Greenbrier Street
Charleston, West Virginia 25311
304-342-1576

Greenbrier County Humane Society
Box 305
Lewisburg, West Virginia 24901
304-536-3535

The Humane Society of Parkersburg
29th & Poplar Road
Parkersburg, West Virginia 26101
304-422-5541

Wisconsin

Fond du Lac Humane Society
237 N. Hickory Street
Fond du Lac, Wisconsin 54935
414-922-8873

Green Bay Humane Society
2206 N. Quincy
Green Bay, Wisconsin 54304
414-435-6150

Rock County Humane Society
222 S. Arch Street
Janesville, Wisconsin 53545
608-752-5622

Kenosha County Humane Society
1307 67th Street
Kenosha, Wisconsin 53140
414-654-0723

Dane County Humane Society
2250 Pennsylvania Avenue
Madison, Wisconsin 53704
608-249-6656

Wisconsin Humane Society
4151 N. Humboldt Avenue
Milwaukee, Wisconsin 53212
414-961-0310

Animal Welfare League

County Trunk G
Neenah, Wisconsin 54956
414-722-9544

Oshkosh Humane Society
815 Dempsy Tr.
Oshkosh, Wisconsin 54901
414-235-4661

Racine County Humane Society
1121 Stuart Road
Racine, Wisconsin 53406
414-886-4497

Sheboygan County Humane Society
3203 N. 15th Street
Sheboygan, Wisconsin 53081
414-458-2012

Watertown Humane Society
Route 3
Watertown, Wisconsin 53094
414-261-1270

Wyoming

(no societies listed in HSUS files)

INDEX